USING SPREADSHEETS EFFECTIV

USING SPREADSHEETS EFFECTIVELY

Gaynor Attwood

McGRAW-HILL BOOK COMPANY

London • New York • St Louis • San Francisco • Auckland
Bogotá • Caracas • Hamburg • Lisbon • Madrid • Mexico
Milan • Montreal • New Delhi • Panama • Paris • San Juan
São Paulo • Singapore • Sydney • Tokyo • Toronto

Published by
McGRAW-HILL Book Company Europe
Shoppenhangers Road, Maidenhead, Berkshire, SL6 2QL, England
Telephone 0628 23432
Fax 0628 770224

British Library Cataloguing-in-Publication Data
Attwood, Gaynor, 1948–
    Using spreadsheets effectively.
    I. Title
    005.369

ISBN 0-07-707295-2

Library of Congress Cataloging-in-Publication Data
Attwood, Gaynor, 1948–
    Using spreadsheets effectively/Gaynor Attwood.
        p.   cm.
    ISBN 0-07-707295-2
    1. Electronic spreadsheets.   I. Title.
HF5548.2.A79   1992
005.3—dc20   91-43284 CIP

Copyright © 1992 McGraw-Hill International (UK) Limited. All rights reserved. No part of this publication may be reproduced, stored in a retrieval system, or transmitted, in any form or by any means, electronic, mechanical, photocopying, recording, or otherwise, without the prior permission of McGraw-Hill International (UK) Limited.
1234 TL9432

Typeset by Oxprint Ltd, Oxford
and printed and bound in Great Britain by
M & A Thomson Litho Ltd, East Kilbride, Scotland

For David and James

CONTENTS

How this book is designed to help you ix

SECTION 1 AN INTRODUCTION TO SPREADSHEETS **1**

- 1.1 What is a spreadsheet? 1
- 1.2 Why use a spreadsheet? 2
- 1.3 What you need to use an electronic spreadsheet 3
- 1.4 Spreadsheet packages currently available 4
- 1.5 How to make comparisons between spreadsheet packages 4

SECTION 2 USING A SPREADSHEET **6**

- 2.1 Creating a spreadsheet 6
- 2.2 Moving around the spreadsheet 6
- 2.3 Entering data 7
- 2.4 Formulas 8
- 2.5 Saving data/reloading data 8
- 2.6 Editing 9
- 2.7 Displaying spreadsheet information 9
- 2.8 Replicating or copying information in a spreadsheet 10
- 2.9 Printing a spreadsheet 11
- 2.10 Other basic spreadsheet features 12
- 2.11 Finishing or quitting a spreadsheet 13
- 2.12 Computer file-handling activities 13
- 2.13 Checklist 14

SECTION 3 ACTIVITIES DESIGNED TO PRACTISE THE BASIC SPREADSHEET ACTIONS **15**

- Learning activity 3.1 15
- Learning activity 3.2 16
- Learning activity 3.3 17
- Learning activity 3.4 18
- Learning activity 3.5 19
- Activity 3.6 20
- Activity 3.7 20
- Activity 3.8 21
- Activity 3.9 21
- Activity 3.10 22

SECTION 4	**FURTHER SPREADSHEET ACTIONS AND FUNCTIONS: I**		**23**
	4.1	Using absolute and relative values	23
	4.2	Sorting information	25
	4.3	Repeating characters to fill a cell	25
	4.4	Protecting and locking cells	25
	4.5	Using date and time functions	25
	4.6	Printing options	26
	4.7	Setting headers and/or footers	27
	4.8	Guidelines for planning and designing spreadsheet layouts	30
	4.9	Creating spreadsheet templates	31
	4.10	Checklist	32
SECTION 5	**ACTIVITIES**		**34**
	Task 5.1		34
	Task 5.2		34
	Task 5.3		35
	Task 5.4		36
	Task 5.5		36
	Task 5.6		37
	Task 5.7		38
	Task 5.8		39
	Task 5.9		40
	Task 5.10		41
SECTION 6	**FURTHER SPREADSHEET ACTIONS AND FUNCTIONS: II**		**43**
	6.1	Producing information in graphic format	43
	6.2	Creating macros	49
	6.3	Naming spreadsheet cells or cell ranges	50
	6.4	Hiding cell contents	50
	6.5	Freezing or fixing worksheet titles, etc.	50
	6.6	Conditions and look-up functions	51
	6.7	Additional functions	52
	6.8	Integrating your spreadsheet with other software applications	53
	6.9	Checklist	53
SECTION 7	**ACTIVITIES**		**54**
	Task 7.1		54
	Task 7.2		54
	Task 7.3		54
	Task 7.4		54
	Task 7.5		55
	Task 7.6		56
	Task 7.7		56
	Task 7.8		57
	Task 7.9		58
	Task 7.10		58
	Task 7.11		59
SECTION 8	**GLOSSARY OF TERMS**		**62**
	INDEX		**67**

HOW THIS BOOK IS DESIGNED TO HELP YOU

The approach used throughout the book is designed to enable you to use spreadsheets on your own computer hardware system with your software.

The book does not give detailed instructions of how your system behaves; it deals with the concepts and skills necessary to make the best use of your hardware and software to carry out those tasks suited to spreadsheets. You will be able to find the information on how your system carries out the functions in your own software handbooks and manuals. By adopting this approach you will be able to transfer your skills from one package to another, and from one version of your software to another.

The book is divided into sections. You will need to decide where you wish to begin your adventure into the use of spreadsheets. Some of you will wish to start at the beginning, read about spreadsheets and then apply your knowledge; others will want to start with some 'hands-on activity' and then read the background material. No one method is best—simply adopt the one that suits you.

I hope you will enjoy using spreadsheets as much as I do.

AN INTRODUCTION TO SPREADSHEETS

SECTION 1

1.1 WHAT IS A SPREADSHEET?

A spreadsheet is a grid of rows and columns that holds information. Computer spreadsheets are a natural development from paper-based spreadsheets. The advantages of using new technology means that you can store and edit the information contained in a spreadsheet quickly and easily, and the size of the spreadsheet can be much larger—but these advantages, and many more, will be more apparent as you become more familiar with your system.

An **electronic spreadsheet** provides a framework for information. The framework is designed so that numbers, text and formula can be entered, edited and stored in an orderly manner.

The framework is a series of boxes in a grid pattern. The lines of boxes down the grid are referred to as **columns** and the lines of boxes across the grid are referred to as **rows** (see Fig. 1.1).

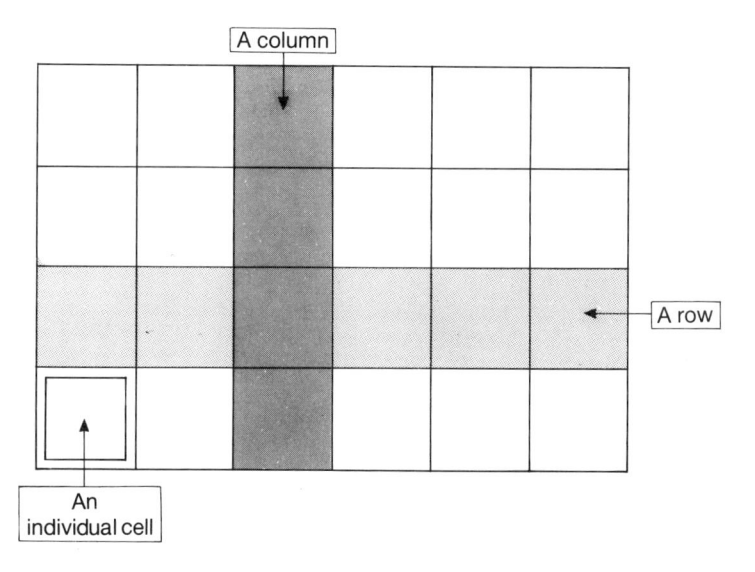

Figure 1.1 Spreadsheet framework showing rows and columns

Each individual box is known as a **cell**.

Each cell on a spreadsheet has an **address**. This is simply a system of describing where exactly that cell can be found, and is achieved by naming both the row and the column. Columns are usually denoted by letters of the alphabet and rows are usually denoted by numbers (see Fig. 1.2).

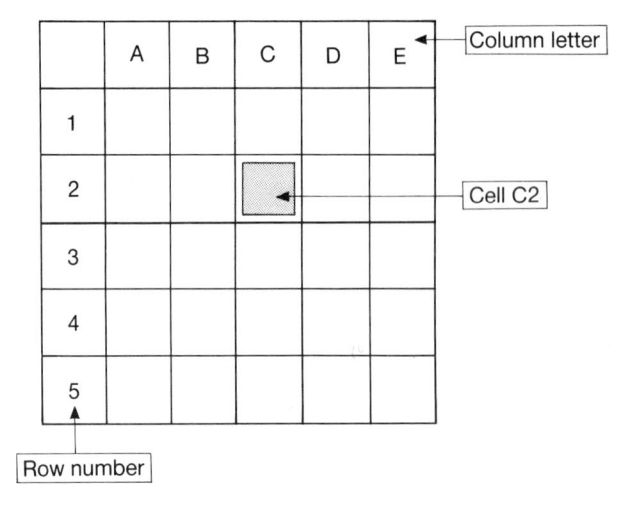

Figure 1.2 Framework showing the address to a cell

Some spreadsheets use numbers for both rows and columns (see Fig. 1.3).

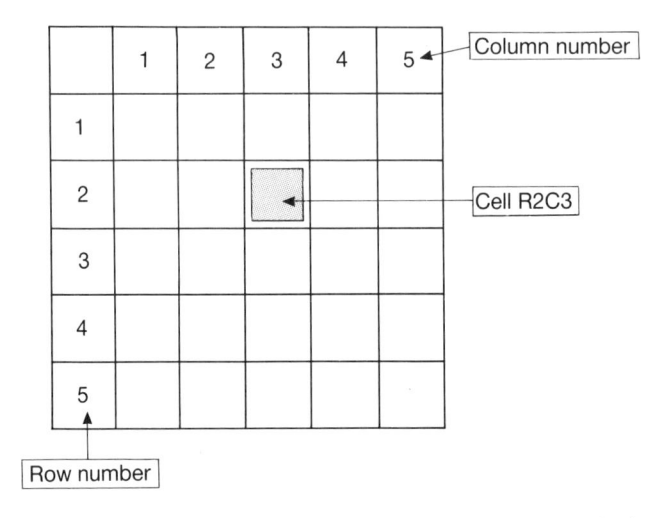

Figure 1.3 Framework in which numbers are used for rows and columns

Spreadsheets will allow you to:
- structure information
- format information
- present information
- edit and update information
- perform calculations
- experiment with the effects of changes in values so that you can make informed decisions.

> *You should now be familiar with these key terms:*
> spreadsheet   row   column   cell   cell address

1.2 WHY USE A SPREADSHEET?

Spreadsheets provide an effective way of displaying and calculating information. The range of uses of a spreadsheet can be said to be limited only by the imagination of the user!!

Some of the more common types of spreadsheets, together with their possible uses, are listed below.

1. *Budget summaries*—e.g. keeping track of a financial situation
2. *Cash flow analysis*—e.g. predicting likely income and expenditure to identify possible financial difficulties
3. *Predicting changes in values*—e.g. working out the effects of a price change, how much price will change if costs increase, effects of discounts, effects of changes in mortgage rates, etc.
4. *General accounting*—e.g. calculating and presenting cash balances, profit and loss accounts, etc.
5. *Business information*—e.g. calculating/estimating, job costing, payment scheduling, payslips, tax records, stock control, forecasting
6. *Analysing financial performance*—e.g. calculating share performance, interest, etc.
7. *Analysing data*—e.g. recording, presenting and analysing results of questionnaires and surveys
8. *Conversion tables*—e.g. performing lists and tables, exchange rates, metric to imperial measurements, Fahrenheit to Celcius
9. *Mathematical techniques*—e.g. calculating, trigonometric and logarithmic functions
10. *Advanced statistic and operational research techniques*—e.g. data analysis, calculating standard deviations, control models, critical path analyses, etc.
11. *Presentation of information*—e.g. presenting numerical data in table format and possibly graphic charts: pie charts, histograms, etc.

1.3 WHAT YOU NEED TO USE AN ELECTRONIC SPREADSHEET

1. **Appropriate computer hardware**
   This will almost certainly need to include a printer and a system of disk storage.

2. **An appropriate software package**
   You will need to consider many factors such as:
   - number of cells available for storing information
   - range of functions offered
   - cost
   - compatibility with your hardware.

   You may wish to read the material presented on page 4, which gives the criteria for comparison of spreadsheet packages. You would be well advised to test any package before purchase, or seek the advice of another user.

3. **A manual or instruction book to accompany your software package**

4. **The information required to prepare the spreadsheet**
   This will be *either* in the format of:

   exercise or task that will enable you to learn about your spreadsheet or how to perform a particular task or function

   or

idea or plan of the information that you will need from the completed spreadsheet, including the layout or format required.

You will also need the information/data required to complete the task.

1.4 SPREADSHEET PACKAGES CURRENTLY AVAILABLE

Many different spreadsheet packages are currently available, and some names may be familiar. The following list gives examples of some of the packages and the hardware systems required.

Lotus 1-2-3	MS.DOS machines
Excel	MS.DOS machines
Supercalc	MS.DOS machines/CPM machine
Multiplan	MS.DOS machines/CPM machine/Nimbus
Grasshopper	Nimbus/BBC
Viewsheet	BBC

1.5 HOW TO MAKE COMPARISONS BETWEEN SPREADSHEET PACKAGES

When you find it necessary to make a decision between packages, you will need to consider the following:

1 What are the hardware requirements?
- Which machine make and type will the package need to operate?
- Will the computer system have enough memory capacity?
- Will the package operate with your printer?

2 What is the size of the spreadsheet in *operational* terms?
- What is the maximum size of the spreadsheet?
- How many rows, how many columns?
- Can you use the maximum number of rows *and* columns, or if you use the maximum number of rows will it reduce the number of columns available, and vice versa?
- How wide can you make the columns?

3 How helpful/friendly is the package?
- Is the handbook readable; if not is there another guide available?
- Is there helpful information displayed on the screen?
- Are the facilities for saving information clear and easy to operate?
- Is the software 'menu' driven?
- Is there a help facility?
- Does the package make use of the special function keys or the mouse?

4 What additional functions are available?
All spreadsheet packages offer basic functions, but this section relates to more than the basic functions. You may like to consider whether your spreadsheet package offers you the opportunity to:

- produce the results of your spreadsheet in graphical form, e.g. pie charts, histograms, scattergraphs
- date the spreadsheet automatically
- print a selected area or just the whole sheet
- arrange to have columns in different widths
- sort the information into numerical and/or alphabetical order
- perform the calculations at speed
- produce advanced mathematical and statistical functions.

What is important now is that you use a spreadsheet.

The material that follows will help you discover, explore and build on your practical spreadsheet skills.

Section 2 has the background information designed to build up the skills required to make effective use of your spreadsheet package.

Section 3 offers a series of learning and consolidation activities relating to basic skills.

Section 4 will help you explore a wider range of spreadsheet functions.

Section 5 offers a further series of learning activities.

Section 6 gives a brief introduction to more advanced spreadsheet functions and techniques.

Section 7 looks at using spreadsheet for problem-solving and decision-making.

Section 8 provides a glossary of terms.

SECTION 2

USING A SPREADSHEET

Whichever spreadsheet you are working with, the basic actions and principles of operation described in the following section will be the same. If you have never used a spreadsheet before, you will need to read this section very carefully. If you have some experience, you may wish to turn to Section 3 to carry out some activities, returning to this section if you encounter any difficulties or need to refer to any points.

2.1 CREATING A SPREADSHEET

Load and enter your spreadsheet package. You may need to give information as to how many columns and rows are required, or your system may simply produce an empty spreadsheet grid ready for your use.

2.2 MOVING AROUND THE SPREADSHEET

As only part of the spreadsheet framework is displayed on the computer screen at any time, the screen provides a window through which you can view any part of the sheet. If you wish to move to an area at present not in view, you will need to **scroll** across to the left or right or **scroll** up or down the spreadsheet. This is usually achieved by moving the cursor or highlight box with the arrow keys or a mouse (see Fig. 2.1).

To help you remember where you are on the spreadsheet, the **current** or **active** cell is displayed and a highlight box usually marks the appropriate cell. The exact placing of this information will depend on the spreadsheet package you are using. Some packages place their status lines above the spreadsheet display; others at the bottom of the screen.

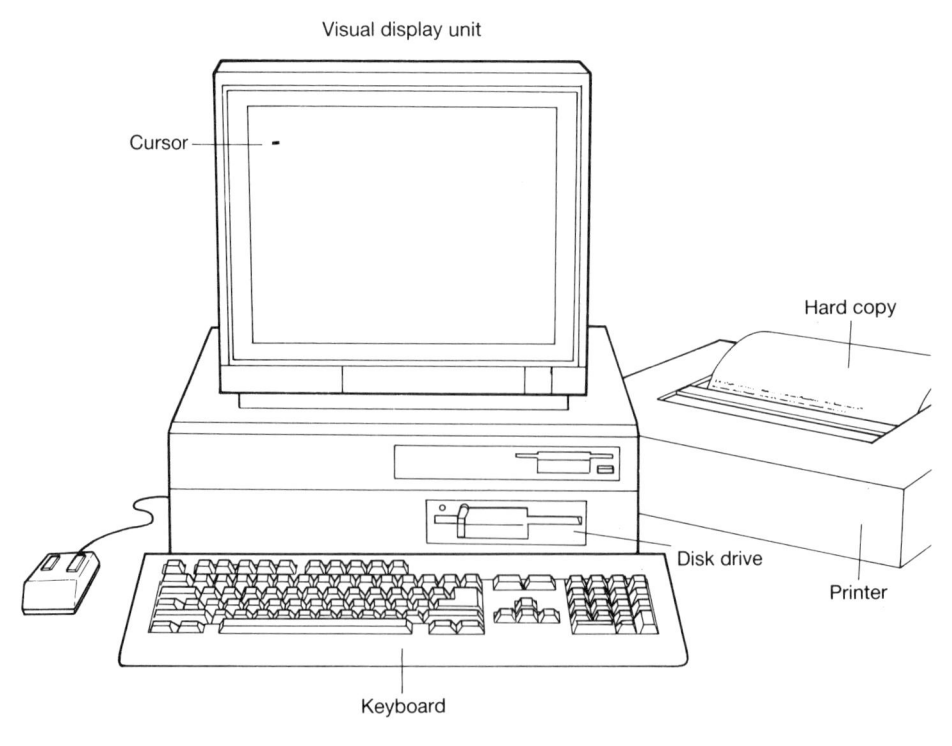

Figure 2.1 Computer screen and system with mouse and keyboard

SECTION 2 • USING SPREADSHEETS EFFECTIVELY

2.3 ENTERING DATA

You can store data in each cell on a spreadsheet (see Fig. 2.2) in one of four ways. You can:

- enter text, or
- enter numbers, or
- enter a formula, or
- leave the cell blank.

With some packages you will need to key in a 'code' before certain entries so that the system can identify the input as text, numbers or formulas. For example: when using Excel, an equals (=) needs to be entered before a formula, and in Lotus 1-2-3 an apostrophe (') before text if it is to be right justified.

Entering text

When text is entered it is normally left justified, i.e. the letters start at the left-hand side of the column.

Entering numbers

When numbers are entered they are normally right justified. You will be able to control the display of the numbers, i.e. whole numbers, decimal points.

Entering a formula

You can enter a formula directly or you may be able to use a special function.

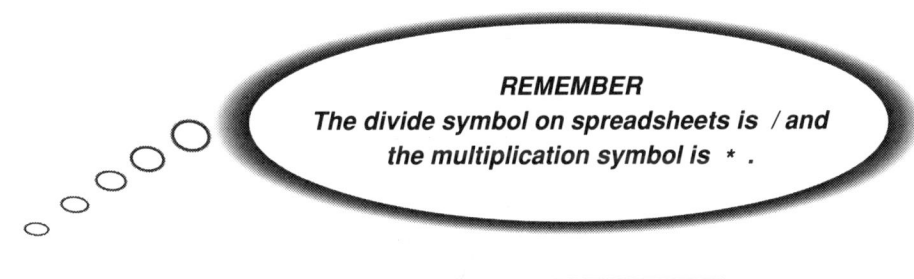

REMEMBER
*The divide symbol on spreadsheets is / and the multiplication symbol is * .*

	A	B	C	D	E
1	INVOICE				
2					
3	Number	Price	Quantity	TOTAL	RUNNING
4		per unit			TOTAL
5					
6	A1003	29.95	3	89.85	89.85
7	B1008	17.50	6	105.00	194.85
8	A1037	8.95	5	44.75	239.60
9	A1431	64.25	2	128.50	368.10

Columns B to E text right justified

A: Text left justified
B: Two fixed decimal places format
C: Integer format
D, E: Two fixed decimal places format

Figure 2.2 Entering data

USING SPREADSHEETS EFFECTIVELY · SECTION 2

2.4 FORMULAS

A formula calculates a new value from existing values.

A formula is made up values, cell references, functions, names or operators.

Parts of a formula

Example 1

$$(B2/3) * 20$$

This formula means that the value stored in cell B2 is divided by 3 and then multiplied by 20.

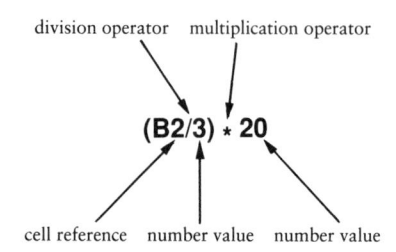

```
        division operator   multiplication operator
                  ↓            ↓
              (B2/3) * 20
               ↑  ↑     ↑
       cell reference  number value  number value
```

Example 2

$$SUM(B1..B2)$$

This formula uses a function SUM to add the values stored in a range of cells from B1 to B12 (including B1 and B12).

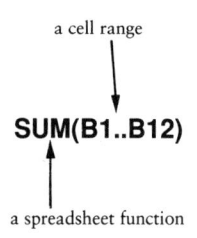

```
              a cell range
                   ↓
            SUM(B1..B12)
             ↑
       a spreadsheet function
```

Example 3

$$\text{wagerate} * \text{hoursworked}$$

This formula is used when certain cells have been given names. In this example the names given are **wagerate** and **hoursworked**. The two values will be multiplied to calculate a new value.

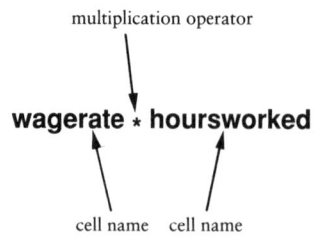

```
         multiplication operator
                  ↓
         wagerate * hoursworked
          ↑              ↑
       cell name     cell name
```

2.5 SAVING DATA / RELOADING DATA

Once any kind of information has been entered it is possible to save, recall and edit the information. It is good practice to save your work frequently. Saving protects your work from being lost in the event of a power or systems failure.

You will need to choose a sensible file name for the work you save as this will help you when you want to recall the information at a later date.

2.6 EDITING

Editing is a powerful feature available on spreadsheets. There are two main ways in which spreadsheet information can be edited.

1 Editing the contents of individual cells

Spreadsheets allow you to delete or change the contents of a cell. To delete information you can either use the delete key or use the blank cell facility. On a spreadsheet any changes to individual number entries will produce an automatic change in totals or calculations that involve that number. For example:

The following information has been entered: in cell A1, 11; in cell A2, 23; and in cell A3, the formula A1 + A2.

	Display on the screen		Contents
	A		A
1	11	1	11
2	23	2	23
3	34	3	A1 + A2

If the entry in cell A2 is altered from 23 to 56, then the result will be as follows:

	Display on the screen		Contents
	A		A
1	11	1	11
2	56	2	56
3	67	3	A1 + A2

The 67 displayed in cell A3 will be the new total automatically calculated as the result of the change of number from 23 to 56 in cell A2.

2 Editing the spreadsheet layout

This can be achieved by inserting or deleting a row or a column on a spreadsheet, as in Fig. 2.3.

	A	B	C	D	E	F	
1	AUTO CARE STORES PLC						Rows 1 and 2 inserted
2							
3	INVOICE						
4							
5	Number	Type	Price	Quantity	TOTAL	RUNNING	
6			per unit			TOTAL	
7							
8	A1003	Tyre	29.95	3	89.85	89.85	← Previous row 8 deleted
9	B1008	Spanner set	17.50	6	105.00	194.85	
10	A1431	Recovery kit	64.25	2	128.50	323.35	

Column B inserted

Figure 2.3 Editing spreadsheet layout

2.7 DISPLAYING SPREADSHEET INFORMATION

You will be able to decide how best to display the information on the spreadsheet. There are three areas to consider.

Text

Text can be placed to the left- or right-hand side of a column; some packages will allow text to be centred over a column.

Numbers

Numbers can be displayed in a variety of ways. For example, as whole numbers (integers), or show decimal places, or be displayed in £.p format. Some packages will allow you to put commas in to mark every thousand, e.g. 1,000,000. Negative numbers will usually be displayed with a minus, e.g. –10, or in brackets, e.g. (10).

> The value entered into a spreadsheet cell is referred to as the stored value, and this will remain as entered; the value that appears on the screen or in a printout of a spreadsheet is the display value.

Overall display

You may be able to select extra functions such as a variety of styles, e.g. bold or italic print, or a variety of fonts. You may be able to vary the column widths or introduce shading to highlight certain areas of the spreadsheet, as in Fig. 2.4.

Main heading in 'Venice' font within a border and background shaded

	A	B	C	D	E	F
1	*AUTO CARE STORES PLC*					
2						
3	INVOICE					
4						
5	Number	Type	Price	Quantity	TOTAL	RUNNING
6			per unit			TOTAL
7						
8	A1003	Tyre	29.95	3	89.85	89.85
9	B1008	Spanner set	17.50	6	105.00	194.85
10	A1431	Recovery kit	64.25	2	128.50	323.35

Headings in bold

Figure 2.4 An example of bold, italic and shading

2.8 REPLICATING OR COPYING INFORMATION IN A SPREADSHEET

Spreadsheets offer you a replication or copying facility. This will allow you to copy information from an existing cell or cells to other locations automatically (see Figs 2.5a and 2.5b). The item replicated can be text, numeric entry or a formula.

	A	B	C	D	E
1	AUTO CARE STORES PLC				
2					
3	INVOICE				
4					
5	Number		Price	Quantity	TOTAL	RUNNING
6			per unit			TOTAL
7						
8	A1003		29.95	3	89.85	89.85
9	B1008		17.50	6	105.00	194.85
10	A1431		64.25	2	128.50	323.35
11	A1321		13.67	5	68.35	391.70
12	C2210		0.87	11	9.57	401.27
13	D3761		4.44	8	35.52	436.79
14	E7860		105.10	2	210.20	646.99

Formula B8 * C8 entered in D8 and replicated down to D14

Formula E8 + D9 entered into E9 and replicated down to E14

Figure 2.5a Replication of numeric entry

	D		E	
3				
4				
5	TOTAL		RUNNING	
6			TOTAL	
7				
8	=B8*C8	Entry	=D8	
9	=B9*C9		=E8+D9	Entry
10	=B10*C10	Replication	=E9+D10	Replication
11	=B11*C11		=E10+D11	
12	=B12*C12		=E11+D12	
13	=B13*C13		=E12+D13	
14	=B14*C14		=E13+D14	
15				
16				

Figure 2.5b Replication of formulas

Most spreadsheets will allow you to copy/replicate information from a single cell or a range of cells.

As you work with spreadsheets you will need to be aware of the difference between abolute and relative values. This aspect of spreadsheet work is covered in Section 4, 4.1, page 23.

....

You will also be able to decide how to print out the information.

2.9 PRINTING A SPREADSHEET

1   You can print out the display (Fig. 2.6), i.e. how the spreadsheet looks when all the calculations and layout instructions have been performed.

AUTO CARE STORES PLC				
INVOICE				
Number	Price	Quantity	TOTAL	RUNNING
	per unit			TOTAL
A1003	29.95	3	89.85	89.85
B1008	17.50	6	105.00	194.85
A1431	64.25	2	128.50	323.35
A1321	13.67	5	68.35	391.70
C2210	0.87	11	9.57	401.27
D3761	4.44	8	35.52	436.79
E7860	105.10	2	210.20	646.99

Display without column and row headings

Figure 2.6 Printout of spreadsheet display

2   You can print the spreadsheet contents (Fig. 2.7), i.e. showing the values and formulas entered in each cell. This may be achieved on a spreadsheet grid or by listing the contents of each cell.

	D	E
3		
4		
5	TOTAL	RUNNING
6		TOTAL
7		
8	=B8*C8	=D8
9	=B9*C9	=E8+D9
10	=B10*C10	=E9+D10
11	=B11*C11	=E10+D11
12	=B12*C12	=E11+D12
13	=B13*C13	=E12+D13
14	=B14*C14	=E13+D14
15		
16		

Spreadsheet contents for columns in the range D3 to E16

Figure 2.7 Printout of spreadsheet contents

2.10 OTHER BASIC SPREADSHEET FEATURES

Some packages will allow you to print out a specific part of the spreadsheet as well as all the information.

....

Other basic commands, functions and actions are available on spreadsheets.

1 Range of cells
A system for identification of a range of cells, e.g. B1..B5 or B1.B5 or B1:B5, would include B1, B2, B3, B4 and B5. This will allow you to determine an area of the spreadsheet to copy, delete, add, etc.

2 Goto
This command allows you to move directly to a specified cell.

3 Functions
A function is a command to carry out a specified instruction. Examples of functions most commonly available are given below. (In the examples, the following values are stored in the cells: A1 = 8, A2 = 9, A3 = 9, A4 = 25, A5 = 4. *Note*: The exact name and example of the function will vary with the package used.)

Function name	Example	Meaning
SUM	SUM(A1..A5)	Will add together result will be 55
AVE	AVE(A1..A5)	Will find the average of numbers in the list A1..A5; result will be 11
MIN	MIN(A1..A5)	Will find the smallest number in the list A1..A5; result will be 4
MAX	MAX(A1..A5)	Will find the largest number in the list A1..A5; result will be 25
COUNT	COUNT(A1..A5)	Will count the number of items in the list A1..A5; result will be 5
SQUARE	SQR(A2)	Will give the square root; the result will be 3

Your spreadsheet software manual will contain more information about the functions available from your package.

4 Calculation speed
If you have a very large spreadsheet with many calculations then there might be a system for turning off the calculation after every cell entry. This will help speed the process of data entry and avoid unnecessary and time-consuming calculations. You must remember to turn the calculation facility on again before studying the results of the spreadsheet or the information supplied will be misleading.

5 What if?
This is using a spreadsheet to consider the effects of a change in the information stored; for example, using a spreadsheet to discover the effects of a *What if* prices rise by 10 per cent, or *What if* the sales fall by 5 per cent. The ability of computers and spreadsheet packages to calculate such changes quickly and efficiently make spreadsheets an extremely valuable decision-making tool.

....

2.11 FINISHING OR QUITTING A SPREADSHEET

Always leave your spreadsheet with the data saved, having exited the package correctly. Make sure that you have duplicate backup copies of important information.

2.12 COMPUTER FILE-HANDLING ACTIVITIES

The more you use spreadsheets the more you will need to consider general computer file-handling activities. These relate to how your spreadsheet data files are stored and managed within your computer system. The information will be available in your hardware and software handbooks and manual.

The following is a checklist of actions you will need to be aware of and, hopefully, be able to perform. It might be helpful to keep a note of how you can achieve these actions with your particular hardware and software combination.

File-handling checklist

I need to know

- **how to format a disk**

This procedure is necessary before you use a new disk with your computer system. You can only use formatted disks to store information.

- **if there are any restrictions or limitations on file names**

Typical restrictions include a limited number of characters, not being able to start a file name with a number, no punctuation, no spaces.

- **how to save files**

This may be a simple instruction within your spreadsheet package.

- **how to list a directory or catalogue of files stored on a disk**

This will enable you to find out which files and computer programs are stored on the disk.

- **how to overwrite existing files**

This will allow you to copy over or update an existing file if you no longer want the original information.

- **how to make backup copies of files**

This means making a second copy of the file preferably on a separate disk. This will provide protection against accidental loss or corruption of information. If your computer system has a hard disk, you should make a second copy of the data on to a floppy disk.

- **how to delete files**

This is necessary when you no longer need a file and wish to remove the information from the disk.

- **how to rename existing files**

This is very useful if you find the name you initially called a file unsuitable; the same information is simply stored under a new name.

2.13 CHECKLIST

Areas covered in Section 2

You should now be familiar with these terms:

- scrolling
- active/current cell
- replication
- spreadsheet contents
- spreadsheet display
- stored values/display values.

You should now have considered how to, and made a note of how to, perform the following actions:

1. Load a spreadsheet package
2. Create a spreadsheet
3. Move the cursor around the spreadsheet
4. Enter text, numbers and formulas
5. Edit a spreadsheet—contents and structure
6. Replicate/copy information within a spreadsheet
7. Save a spreadsheet
8. Reload a spreadsheet
9. Print a spreadsheet
10. A number of file-handling activities:
    - format a disk
    - save a file
    - list the directory or catalogue the disk
    - overwrite an existing file
    - delete a file
    - rename a file.

ACTIVITIES DESIGNED TO PRACTISE THE BASIC SPREADSHEET ACTIONS

SECTION 3

The following activities are designed to help you understand the **basic** principles of using a spreadsheet package. Use your software and hardware manual and instruction books to help you find out how your system works.

The spreadsheet actions are introduced in the following learning activities:

Action	Learning acivity
Loading the package	3.1
Quitting the package	3.1
Create a spreadsheet framework	3.1
Entering data—numbers	3.1
Entering data—text	3.1
Entering data—formula	3.2
Saving spreadsheet data/file	3.1
Loading spreadsheet data file	3.2
Moving the cursor	3.1
Editing data	3.2
Changing format—text: left	3.4
Changing format—text: right	3.4
Changing format—text: centre	3.5
Changing format—numbers: £.p (two fixed decimal places)	3.4
Changing format—numbers: integer	3.5
Changing format—numbers: decimals	3.5
Changing column width	3.4
Insert/delete row	3.4
Insert/delete column	3.5
Replicate or copy a cell or range of cells	3.2
Goto a particular cell	3.5
Printing a spreadsheet: display	3.1
Printing a spreadsheet: contents	3.5

You will need to know how to:
- power up your hardware system
- load the spreadsheet program
- enter text and numbers
- create a spreadsheet framework
- save the spreadsheet data
- print the spreadsheet display

LEARNING ACTIVITY 3.1

Requirements

You are going to prepare a spreadsheet to calculate the number of holiday brochures requested during the month of January. You need to find out how many brochures are required each week and how many on each day; you also need the total for the month.

1   Switch on your system and load your spreadsheet program.

2. Create a spreadsheet to hold the following information (note you will require a minimum of seven columns and six rows).

Week	Mon	Tues	Wed	Thurs	Fri
1	100	82	30	80	73
2	27	78	20	85	49
3	53	100	50	92	60
4	60	20	60	51	83

3. Enter the data into your spreadsheet.
4. Proofread the data and correct any mistakes.
5. Save the spreadsheet file.
6. Print the spreadsheet.

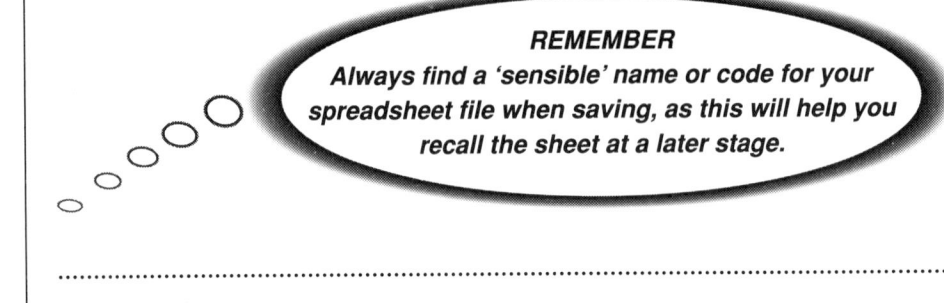

> **REMEMBER**
> Always find a 'sensible' name or code for your spreadsheet file when saving, as this will help you recall the sheet at a later stage.

LEARNING ACTIVITY 3.2

You will need to know how to:
- load a spreadsheet file
- enter formulas
- replicate/copy
- edit data

1. Reload the spreadsheet saved in Learning Activity 3.1.
2. Insert the heading **Total** in the two places shown:

Week	Mon	Tues	Wed	Thurs	Fri	Total
1						
2						
3						
4						
Total	***					

3. Create and position a formula where *** is shown. The formula will add the figures for Monday week 1, Monday week 2, Monday week 3 and Monday week 4.

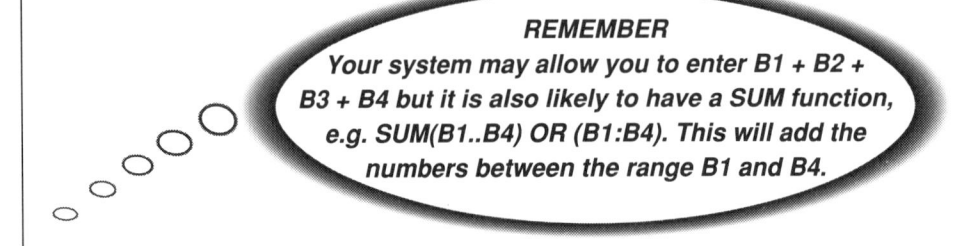

> **REMEMBER**
> Your system may allow you to enter B1 + B2 + B3 + B4 but it is also likely to have a SUM function, e.g. SUM(B1..B4) OR (B1:B4). This will add the numbers between the range B1 and B4.

SECTION 3 · USING SPREADSHEETS EFFECTIVELY

4   Use your spreadsheet package to copy or replicate the formula created in step 3 so that the totals are given for Tuesday, Wednesday, Thursday and Friday.

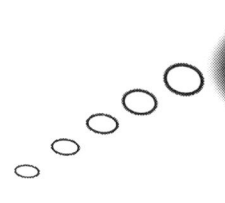

> **REMEMBER**
> The copy or replicate function allows you to copy the contents from one cell or a range of cells to another part of the spreadsheet without the need to re-enter the data.

5   Now total the brochures requested during week 1—that is, add the figures for Monday, Tuesday, Wednesday, Thursday and Friday—and place that figure in the appropriate total cell.

6   Replicate the formula created in step 5 for weeks 2, 3, 4 and the overall total.

7   As you were given an incorrect figure for Tuesday week 2 you will need to edit the data. The figure you should enter is 85.

8   Save your spreadsheet. Print your spreadsheet.

In this section you will consolidate the various actions required for Learning Activities 3.1 and 3.2

LEARNING ACTIVITY 3.3

Requirements

From the following information you will need to find the total marks for each student and the average mark for each test.

1   Create a spreadsheet to hold the following information:

Student	Test 1	Test 2	Test 3	Total
Williams P	60	15	52	
Croll P	80	30	12	
Feather D	33	46	24	
Ridley M	29	79	23	
Richards H	58	77	85	
Average				

2   Enter the data into your spreadsheet.

3   Enter the formula to total P Williams's marks. Replicate the formula for the other students.

4   Save the spreadsheet.

5   Create a formula to average the marks for Test 1; this will be the total marks scored divided by the number of students. Copy the formula for Test 2 and Test 3.

6   Save and print the spreadsheet.

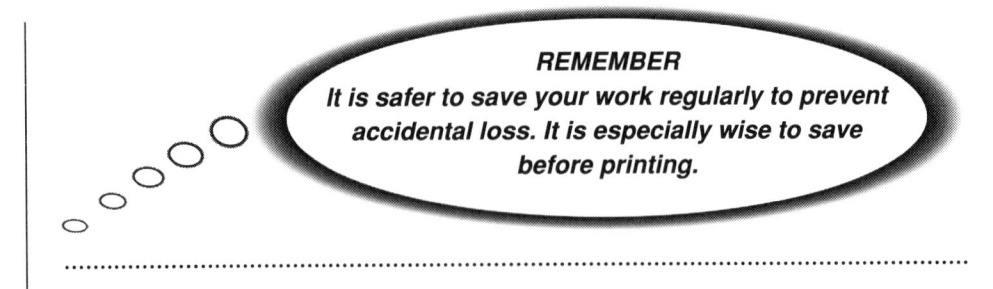

LEARNING ACTIVITY 3.4

> **REMEMBER**
> It is safer to save your work regularly to prevent accidental loss. It is especially wise to save before printing.

You will need to know how to:
- insert a row
- change column width
- format text to left and right of cells
- format numbers in £.p format (two fixed decimal places)

Requirements

You are to prepare a spreadsheet to show the total cost of the purchase of a number of rugby shirts. You will also need to display the total purchase price.

1. Load your spreadsheet package and create a framework to hold the information that follows:

Item	Price per item	No. required	Price
England	12.90	10	
Wales	13.05	13	
Scotland	12.80	12	
Ireland	13.05	7	
British Lions	13.25	6	
France	12.95	8	

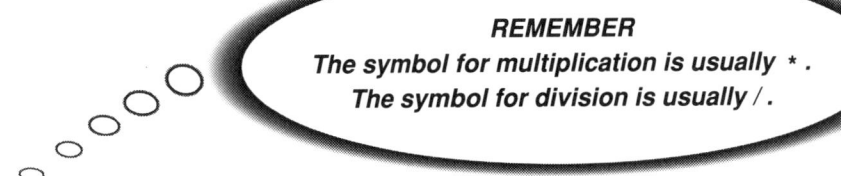

> **REMEMBER**
> The symbol for multiplication is usually *.
> The symbol for division is usually /.

2. Enter the information.

3. Create a formula to find the total price for the number of England rugby shirts required.

4. Replicate this formula for the other rugby shirts and extend the formula to produce an overall total.

5. Save and print the spreadsheet.

6. You need to consider the presentation of this information. Look at your printout and then try some, or all, of the following:

   (a) Make sure all the text in column 1 is justified to the left.
   (b) Ensure that the headings in columns 2, 3 and 4 are justified to the right.
   (c) Ensure that the display in columns 2 and 4 is displayed with two fixed decimal places (£.p format). The information in column 3 should be in integer (whole number) format.

7. Save and print the spreadsheet. Compare this printout with the printout produced at step 5.

LEARNING ACTIVITY 3.5

You will need to know how to:
- move or *goto* a particular cell
- change number format to integer
- change number format to decimal places
- insert/delete a column
- centre text
- print spreadsheet contents

Requirements

You are considering puchasing several notice boards. The information in the catalogue is not as helpful as you would wish. Set up a spreadsheet to calculate the cost per square centimetre of the various sizes of notice boards.

PINBOARDS COMPLETE WITH FIXING CLIPS

Dimensions	Cat. No.	Price	Colours
60 × 60 cm	64PL	27.50	All
60 × 90 cm	64PM	31.90	All
60 × 120 cm	64PN	36.30	All
90 × 120 cm	64PO	48.40	All
120 × 120 cm	64PP	60.50	All
120 × 150 cm	64PQ	71.50	All
120 × 180 cm	64PR	81.95	Wheat
120 × 240 cm	64PS	104.50	Wheat

* When ordering please state colour required.
* Where a choice is available, select from: wheat, claret, cereal, barley, saffron, spice or nutmeg.
* If you require special sizes or colours please contact tele-sales for a quotation.

Figure 3.1 Pinboard advertisement

1. Set up a spreadsheet to show the information given in Fig. 3.1. Suggested headings for the columns could be: *Cat. No.*, *Length*, *Width*, *Colour* and *Cost*.

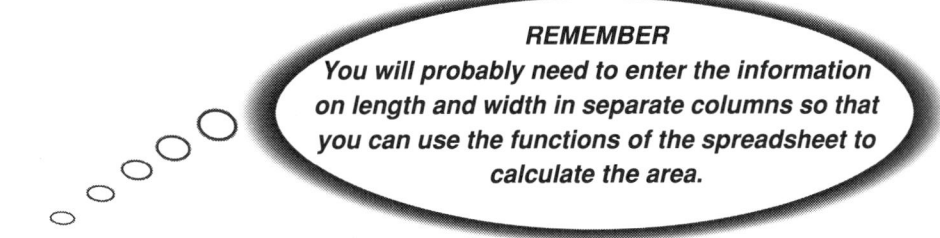

> **REMEMBER**
> **You will probably need to enter the information on length and width in separate columns so that you can use the functions of the spreadsheet to calculate the area.**

2. Enter the information given in the figure.
3. Set up a sixth column to calculate the area. The formula required will be the length of the board multiplied by the width.
4. If you have not already done so, save the information.

USING SPREADSHEETS EFFECTIVELY • SECTION 3

5 The next stage is to calculate the cost per square centimetre. Under the appropriate heading, enter the formula (area divided by cost).

6 Save and print the information.

7 Study the printout, and try the following improvements in layout of the information:

   - centre the text headings over the columns (if you cannot do this with your software package then right-justify the headings)
   - display the information relating to price in integer format
   - display the information relating to cost per square centimetre, showing two decimal places.

8 Save the information.

9 Delete the column containing the information relating to the colours available.

10 Save and print the spreadsheet. You require two printouts: the first of the display; the second of the contents so that you can use this for reference later.

ACTIVITY 3.6

You need to create a spreadsheet to calculate the volumes of a number of boxes. You are given details for 12 boxes. The height of all boxes is 5 cm. The bases of the boxes are as follows:

2 × 2 cm	3 × 2 cm	4 × 4 cm	5 × 5 cm
2 × 3 cm	3 × 3 cm	4 × 5 cm	5 × 6 cm
2 × 4 cm	3 × 4 cm	4 × 6 cm	6 × 6 cm

(To calculate the volume multiply the base by the height.)

1 Provide a spreadsheet to perform the calculations and give a suitable main heading and column headings.

2 Enter the height for this first box and then use the replicate facility to enter the height for the other boxes. The replicate facility can also be used to copy the formula.

ACTIVITY 3.7

You are required to find the average mark for a group of students. Each student has completed five assignments. Put the students' names in the first column, the assignment scores in the next five columns and the average score in column seven.

The information on the students' scores is as follows:

Dry S	20	15	13	16	18
Kewell T	18	17	14	18	12
Groves M	12	13	10	11	17
Saunders S	18	12	16	19	15
Martyres A	10	11	13	9	14
Kumar L	19	18	13	15	18

Display the average figure to two decimal places. The names in column 1 should be left justified, headings in columns 2 to 7 should be right justified.

(To check that your formula is correct, the average score for S Dry will be 16.40.)

> **REMEMBER**
> *Your spreadsheet package may have a function to calculate average.*

1. Provide a printout showing the average scores.

2. You are requested to show the average scores as whole numbers (integer format).

3. An error has occurred with the test scores for assignment five, reduce all scores by three marks.

4. Provide a printout showing these amendments.

....

ACTIVITY 3.8

Create and produce a spreadsheet layout to calculate the total cost of photo-copying for the year.

There will be six columns: column 1 will show the months, column 2 will show the opening numbers, column 3 the closing numbers, column 4 the numbers used. The fifth column will show the unit cost at 2.1p per copy and the sixth column will show the total cost for each month (number used multiplied by the unit cost).

The following information is supplied:

Month	Opening number	Closing number	Numbers used	Unit cost	Total
Jan	1,003	2,065			
Feb	2,065	2,987			
March	2,987	3,642			
April	3,642	7,100			
May	7,100	8,234			
June	8,234	9,173			
July	9,173	10,821			
Aug	10,821	12,399			
Sept	12,399	12,506			
Oct	12,506	13,610			
Nov	13,610	14,837			
Dec	14,837	16,210			

In the row after December show the **Total** cost for the year. (This will be the total of the costs for each month.)

Save the file under a suitable name. Print a copy of the file. Check the printout and amend the layout if necessary.

....

ACTIVITY 3.9

You are required to produce a spreadsheet to show whether the departmental funds of the local school—Firwood School—are underspent or overspent for the year.

The departments are as follows:

(1) Humanities; (2) Art; (3) Science; (4) Mathematics; (5) Technology;

(6) English; (7) Modern Languages.

The allocations for each department, in £s, are:

(1) 800.00;   (2) 450.00;   (3) 1,200.00;   (4) 900.00;
(5) 850.00;   (6) 650.00;   (7) 350.00.

The expenditure to date for each department, in £s, is:

(1) 372.89;   (2) 469.87;   (3) 1,191.43;   (4) 725.00;
(5) 518.02;   (6) 827.00;   (7) 349.05.

1. Use the above information to produce a spreadsheet to show the amount of overspend/underspend.

2. List the departments in column 1, the allocations in column 2 and the expenditure in column 3. Produce the formula to show the overspend or underspend in column 4. Use suitable column heading where appropriate. Do not insert the bracketed numbers.

3. Produce a printout of the completed worksheet.

4. Add a row (below Modern Languages) to show the **Total** for monies allocated, monies spent, and the balance of the overspend/underspend.

ACTIVITY 3.10

The owner of a small business—The Gift Shop—needs a spreadsheet to show the selling price of goods.

The selling price is to be calculated by taking cost price and adding a 10 per cent mark-up.

The items and the cost prices are as follows:

	£ per unit		£ per unit
China horse	21.00	Paperweight	56.00
China figurine	13.00	Pen set	8.45
Brass vases	6.00	Leather wallet	10.60
Crystal dolphin	11.00	Leather purse	11.20
Crystal eagle	11.00	Ship's brass bell	6.50
Porcelain plate	12.50	Shoe clean kit	6.80
Porcelain vase	11.50	Penknife	13.49

1. Design and set up a spreadsheet for the owner.

2. Suggested column headings: *Item, Cost price, Mark-up 10%, Selling price*.

3. Save and print a copy of the spreadsheet.

4. Check the presentation of the information and amend as necessary.

5. Save the file and print a copy for the shop's owner.

6. The owner would now like to consider the selling price if mark-up was 15 per cent.

7. Reload the spreadsheet file and add two further columns to show *Mark-up 15%* and *Selling price*.

8. Save the file and print a copy of the sheet.

FURTHER SPREADSHEET ACTIONS AND FUNCTIONS: I

SECTION 4

Once you feel confident with the basic spreadsheet skills you will be ready to explore further.

In this section there will be a short explanation of a range of spreadsheet actions and functions that will allow you to build on the basic skills introduced in Section 2.

The actions and functions introduced in this section provide you with the opportunity to consider how you might be able to perform these with your spreadsheet system. Remember, you may not be able to perform all the actions/functions covered due to the limitations of your software package.

4.1 USING ABSOLUTE AND RELATIVE CELL REFERENCES

When setting up a spreadsheet you need to appreciate the difference between absolute and relative values. This is particularly important when you are using the replicate or copy facility.

On most spreadsheets the numeric values you enter will be relative references unless you specify otherwise.

- When a **relative** value is copied or replicated, all references to that cell are changed in relation to the new cell reference.
- When an **absolute** value is copied or replicated, any reference to that cell is not changed and will always refer to the value in the cell reference entered.

This is best explained by use of an example, as Fig. 4.1, which demonstrates the effects of replicating a **relative** value.

	A	B	C	D
1		Jan	Feb	March
2	Till 1	100	20	
3	Till 2	200	400	
4	Till 3	100	156	
5	Total	SUM(B2..B4)	SUM(C2..C4)	SUM(D2..D4)

Figure 4.1 Replicating a relative value

The reference entered in cell B5 for B2, B3 and B4 was **relative**. When the formula was copied to C5 and D5, the references automatically change to C2, C3 and C4 and D2, D3 and D4.

The second example (Fig. 4.2) demonstrates where it would be appropriate to use both **absolute** and **relative** cell references. The following spreadsheet is set up to calculate the wage payable to staff when the number of hours worked is known and the wage rate is known. The information relating to the numbers of hours worked by each person will vary for each worker, whereas the rate of pay per hour is the same for all workers.

USING SPREADSHEETS EFFECTIVELY • SECTION 4

Notes on Fig. 4.2

1. The rate of pay is shown in cell B2.

2. The column headings are:
   Name (cell A4); *No. of hours worked* (cells B4 and B5); *Pay due* (cell C4).

3. The rate of pay and number of hours worked are numeric entries.

4. The formula has been entered in C6. The formula to calculate the pay due is the number of hours worked multiplied by the rate of pay.

5. The number of hours worked is a relative value; as it is copied down the column for pay due, it will change for each worker B6, to B7, ... to B10.

6. The rate of pay is an absolute cell reference (B2); as it is copied down the spreadsheet it will remain unchanged.

Look at the spreadsheet contents and display in Figs 4.2 and 4.3, respectively.

SPREADSHEET CONTENTS

	A	B	C
1	PART TIME HOURLY PAY ACCOUNT		
2	RATE OF PAY = £	15.00	
3			
4	NAME	NO. OF HOURS	PAY DUE
5		WORKED	
6	Collins P	20	B6 * B2
7	Richard C	12	B7 * B2
8	Hammer M C	14	B8 * B2
9	Donovan J	12	B9 * B2
10	Mercury F	8	B10 * B2

C6: directly entered; C7–C10: replicated

- information in B2 is an absolute value
- information B6 to B10 has relative values
- information in C6 to C10 is a mixed cell reference as the number of hours is relative value the rate of pay is absolute value

Figure 4.2 Spreadsheet contents

SPREADSHEET DISPLAY

	A	B	C
1	PART TIME HOURLY PAY ACCOUNT		
2	RATE OF PAY = £	15.00	← (No. of hrs worked * Rate of pay)
3			
4	NAME	NO. OF HOURS	PAY DUE
5		WORKED	
6	Collins P	20	300.00
7	Richard C	12	180.00
8	Hammer M C	14	210.00
9	Donovan J	12	180.00
10	Mercury F	8	120.00

Figure 4.3 Spreadsheet display

SECTION 4 • USING SPREADSHEETS EFFECTIVELY

7   The cell references relating to the formula in the 'pay due' column (column C) in Fig. 4.3 could be described as mixed cell references as they contain both a relative and an absolute value.

> The precise method for entering absolute values will depend on the spreadsheet package you are using. For example, with Excel and Lotus 1-2-3 you must put a '$' before the cell reference, e.g. B3 for an absolute reference. Some packages will allow you to identify both the row and column.

4.2 SORTING INFORMATION

Computers can sort information in either numerical order or alphabetical order. If your spreadsheet makes use of this facility, then this will allow you to produce information such as customer or employee lists in alphabetical order or produce information in numerical order, such as job code or salary. You will need to define the area of your spreadsheet to be sorted. Remember, this needs to be done very carefully; you will not want to include headings or other such information in the sort. You will also need to include all related information otherwise you might only sort one column and the result would be that its related information would be in the wrong sequence.

4.3 REPEATING CHARACTERS TO FILL A CELL

Most spreadsheet packages have a system that enables you to repeat a single character to fill the width of a cell. This feature is commonly used to produce lines across a spreadsheet, as shown in Fig. 4.4.

	A	B	C	D
1		Jan	Feb	Mar
2	Sales	61000	58000	65000
3	Marketing	20000	15000	20000
4	Finance	10000	12000	10000
5	---
6	Total	91000	85000	85000
7	===

Figure 4.4   Replicating characters to fill a cell

If you were using Lotus 1-2-3 then at A5 in Fig. 4.4 you would enter backslash (\) – and at A7 backslash (\) =. To rule across several cells simply replicate from the first cell as necessary.

4.4 PROTECTING AND LOCKING CELLS

This is a particularly useful function when formulas or data have been entered on your spreadsheet and you do not wish to change or overwrite them without careful thought. When a cell is locked you will not be allowed to change the information in that cell without unlocking it first.

Your package might allow you to protect or lock an individual cell, a range of cells or the whole sheet. Access to the whole sheet would then only be available by use of a password.

4.5 USING DATE AND TIME FUNCTIONS

As many computers have a 'real time' clock, this feature is often made available to you by spreadsheet package designers. If your hardware and software combination allows you to use this function, you will be able to date and time your spreadsheet printouts automatically.

You must first place the appropriate code in the cell, and the code will then be converted into the date (Fig. 4.5a) and/or time (Fig. 4.5b) when printed. You will normally be able to select the exact display or format of the information.

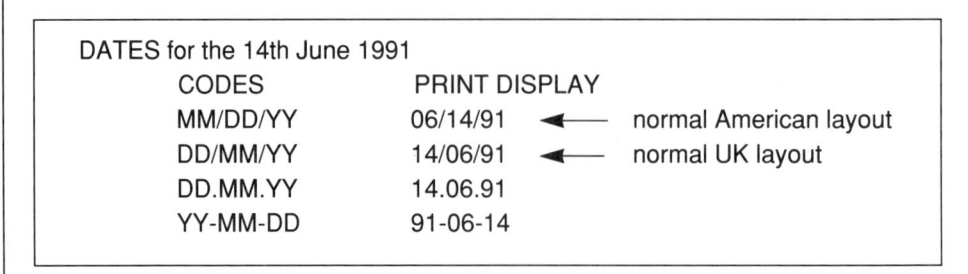

```
DATES for the 14th June 1991
    CODES           PRINT DISPLAY
    MM/DD/YY        06/14/91      ◀——  normal American layout
    DD/MM/YY        14/06/91      ◀——  normal UK layout
    DD.MM.YY        14.06.91
    YY-MM-DD        91-06-14
```

Figure 4.5a   Date function

```
TIMES for 35 minutes and 5 seconds past 11 in the morning
    CODES           PRINT DISPLAY
    HH.MM.SS.       11.30.05    or 11.30
    HH:MM:SS        11:30:05    or 11:30
    HH,MM,SS        11,30,5     or 11,30
    HHhMMmSSs       11h30m05s   or 11h30m
```

Figure 4.5b   Time function

The following shows the entries for a spreadsheet printed on 14 June 1991.

	A	B
1	CASH FLOW ANALYSIS	
2	information printed:	@TODAY

The layout option selected was DD/MM/YY, which will produce the display:

	A	B
1	CASH FLOW ANALYSIS	
2	information printed:	14/06/91

4.6 PRINTING OPTIONS

Your spreadsheet will offer you choices as to the range and type of printouts available.

You have already considered how to print out the spreadsheet **contents** and the spreadsheet **display** and whether your system will print with a variety of **fonts** and/or shading.

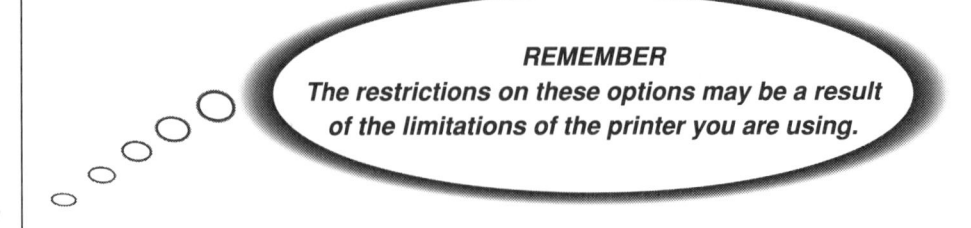

> **REMEMBER**
> *The restrictions on these options may be a result of the limitations of the printer you are using.*

On your system you may also be able to control where to start a new page, i.e. enter a page break, and to select whether to print:

- the borders on or off (Fig. 4.6a)
- the grid on or off (Fig. 4.6b)
- part of the spreadsheet.

Heading boxed
and background
shaded

Times font bold
display font

ASSESSMENT TEST RESULTS

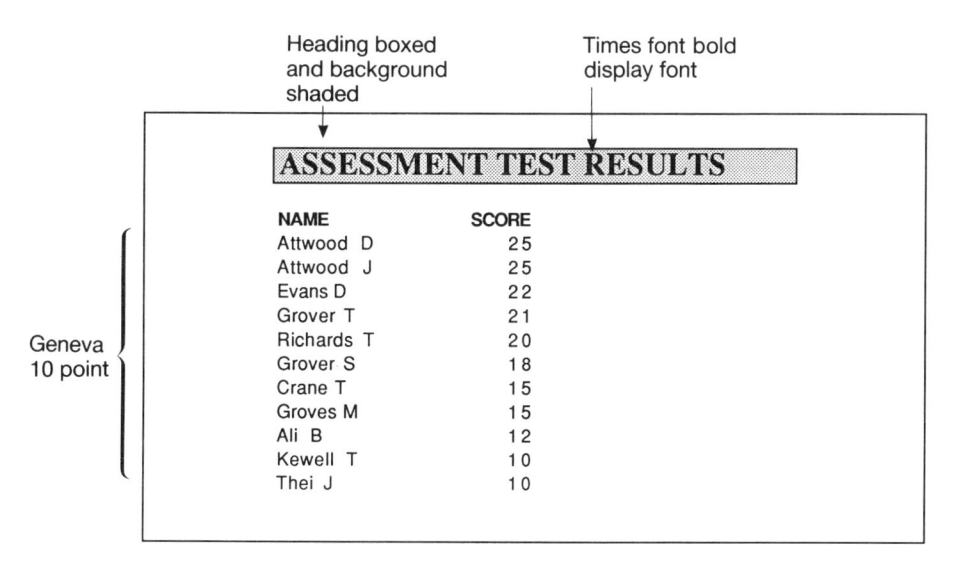

NAME	SCORE
Attwood D	25
Attwood J	25
Evans D	22
Grover T	21
Richards T	20
Grover S	18
Crane T	15
Groves M	15
Ali B	12
Kewell T	10
Thei J	10

Geneva 10 point

Figure 4.6a Information with grid lines off and an outside border

	A	B	C	D	E
1	ASSESSMENT TEST RESULTS				
2					
3	NAME	SCORE			
4	Attwood D	25			
5	Attwood J	25			
6	Evans D	22			
7	Grover T	21			
8	Richards T	20			
9	Grover S	18			
10	Crane T	15			
11	Groves M	15			
12	Ali B	12			
13	Kewell T	10			
14	Thei J	10			
15					
16					

Figure 4.6b Information with grid lines on

4.7 SETTING HEADERS AND/OR FOOTERS

Some packages will allow you to print a line or two on each page of the spreadsheet above and/or below the spreadsheet grid. The information above the spreadsheet is referred to as a **header** and the information below the spreadsheet is referred to as a **footer** (see Fig. 4.7a).

The information contained usually refers to:

- the file name of the spreadsheet
- the name of the person preparing the spreadsheet (Fig. 4.7b)
- the title of the spreadsheet (Fig. 4.7b)
- the date and/or time the spreadsheet was printed (Fig. 4.7b)
- the page numbers. (These are produced automatically and can be very useful if your spreadsheet is longer than a single page; you will enter a code and the package will enter the appropriate page number.)

One minor point to note is that a header or footer may not appear on the screen, but will only appear when the spreadsheet data are printed out. You will find that if your spreadsheet package offers this function then you will need to know the appropriate codes and commands.

This is a header

	A	B	C	D	E	F
1						
2						
3						
4						
5						
6						
7						
8						
9						
10						
11						
12						
13						
14						
15						
16						
17						
18						
19						
20						
21						
22						
23						
24						
25						
26						
27						
28						
29						
30						
31						
32						
33						
34						
35						
36						
37						
38						
39						
40						
41						
42						
43						
44						
45						
46						

This is a footer

Figure 4.7a Example of header and footer

Profit and Loss Account { File name used as header

	A	B	C	D	E	F
1						
2						
3						
4						
5						
6						
7						
8						
9						
10						
11						
12						
13						
14						
15						
16						
17						
18						
19						
20						
21						
22						
23						
24						
25						
26						
27						
28						
29						
30						
31						
32						
33						
34						
35						
36						
37						
38						
39						
40						
41						
42						
43						
44						
45						
46						

Footer — Page 1   prepared by A N Other at 11:33 AM

- Page number
- Information
- Time printed (could add date)

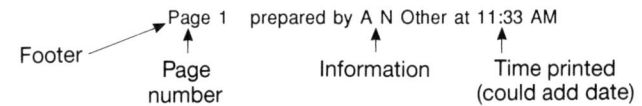

Figure 4.7b   Example of filled-in header and footer

4.8 GUIDELINES FOR PLANNING AND DESIGNING SPREADSHEET LAYOUTS

You are advised to adopt the following guidelines when planning a spreadsheet.

1. 'Map' your spreadsheet on paper and keep an updated layout plan.

2. Keep the design as simple as possible.

3. Make the spreadsheet easy for other users to understand.

4. Choose a sensible layout:
   - include column and row headings
   - use a main heading
   - use rulings
   - decide on the placing of text—left or right justified or centred
   - decide on the display for numbers—whole numbers, £.p format or how many fixed places to set decimals.

5. Keep documentation to help you remember why you set up your spreadsheet in a particular format and to help you plan any future amendments. Keep a printout of the final sheet and its contents for reference.

6. Use validation tests if possible—these will be check routines to make sure your formulas are correctly entered.

7. Test your spreadsheet before you use it! Be prepared to modify your spreadsheet layout after the trial if necessary.

8. Plan which cells might need protecting or locking on your spreadsheet.

9. Decide on a sensible file name for saving, and make provision for backup copies.

A template is a spreadsheet that contains structure—headings, formulas, layout information, headers and/or footers—but no data. A template is set up in advance (Fig. 4.8a) and is then completed with the appropriate data as they become available (Fig. 4.8b)

4.9 CREATING SPREADSHEET TEMPLATES

Part-time Staffing Expenditure

	B	C
1		
2		
3		
4		
5		
6		
7	Hours	Cost
8	Worked	
9		=payrate*B9
10		=payrate*B10
11		=payrate*B11
12		=payrate*B12
13		=payrate*B13
14		=payrate*B14
15		=payrate*B15
16		=payrate*B16
17		=payrate*B17
18		=payrate*B18
19		=payrate*B19
20		=payrate*B20
21		
22		
23		
24		
25		
26		
27		
28		
29		
30		
31		
32		
33		
34		
35		
36		
37		
38		
39		
40		
41		
42		
43		
44		
45		
46		
47		

Page 1

Figure 4.8a Contents of template spreadsheet

	A	B	C
1	PART-TIME STAFFING EXPENDITURE		
2			
3	For the period ending:		
4			
5	Current Hourly Rate of Pay		
6			
7	NAME	Hours	Cost
8		Worked	
9			0
10			0
11			0
12			0
13			0
14			0
15			0
16			0
17			0
18			0
19			0
20			0

— Cell B5 named as payrate

— Formula entered payrate * B7

Formula replicated as far as necessary

FORMAT INFORMATION
Column width (default = 10 characters)
Column A set to   20 characters
Column B and C set to   8 characters

Text left justified.

Number format in columns B and C set to two fixed decimal places (£.p) format

Figure 4.8b Template filled with data

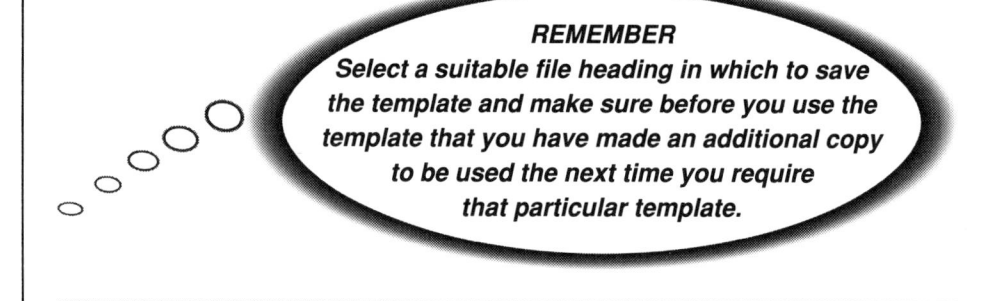

> **REMEMBER**
> Select a suitable file heading in which to save the template and make sure before you use the template that you have made an additional copy to be used the next time you require that particular template.

4.10 CHECKLIST

Areas covered in Section 4

After working through this section you should now have discovered if your package offers the range of facilities listed below; if so, you should have considered how to perform them.

1 Insert a relative cell reference in a formula.

2 Insert an absolute cell reference in a formula.

3 Sort information numerically in ascending and descending order.

4 Sort information alphabetically.

5 Rule lines across a spreadsheet using cell fill functions.

6 Protect and lock cells.

7 Enter a date function.

8 Enter a time function.

9 Print a spreadsheet with column letters and row numbers showing the grid on.

10 Print part of the spreadsheet.

11 Enter a header.

12 Enter a footer.

You should also be able to indentify the main stages in:

- planning and designing a spreadsheet
- designing and creating a spreadsheet template.

SECTION 5

ACTIVITIES

TASK 5.1

Part 1

You are required to produce a spreadsheet to show the costs of the Happy Spanner Works.

The information supplied is

Output (000s)	Fixed costs	Variable costs
1	2,000	3,500
2	2,000	5,600
3	2,000	7,400
4	2,000	10,000
5	2,000	14,000
6	2,000	20,000
7	2,000	28,500
8	2,000	39,600

The information that must be calculated at each level of output is:

Total cost   Marginal cost   Average cost

The formulas needed are:

- Total cost = Fixed cost plus variable cost
- Average cost = Total cost divided by output
- Marginal cost = The additional cost of producing the last unit of output

Present the information as attractively as possible. Save your spreadsheet file.

Part 2

Due to an increase in rent and the business community charge, fixed costs are set to increase by 10 per cent whereas variable costs are to increase by 5 per cent. Recall your file from Part 1 and make the amendments.

1 Save this spreadsheet under a new name so that you have copies of the spreadsheet from Part 1 and Part 2.

2 Print a copy of your spreadsheet.

TASK 5.2

Part 1

You are required to produce a spreadsheet to show the selling price of the products for sale. You are given the cost price and you must add VAT. The current rate of VAT is 17.5 per cent for all items sold but this could change in the future.

The 12 products and their cost prices are as follows:

Product A	£100.00	Product E	£75.00	Product I	£0.50
Product B	£20.00	Product F	£85.00	Product J	£100.00
Product C	£30.00	Product G	£15.00	Product K	£32.00
Product D	£55.00	Product H	£4.00	Product L	£20.00

Set up the spreadsheet with an appropriate title and with suitable column headings and row titles.

Part 2

You are now given information relating to the number of goods sold of each product.

Product A	12	Product E	5	Product I	500
Product B	72	Product F	2	Product J	11
Product C	20	Product G	20	Product K	7
Product D	33	Product H	100	Product L	8

The layout of the spreadsheet needs to be modified to show the total income from sales (cost multiplied by the number sold) the VAT charges on all items sold (total income multiplied by the VAT payable) and the total income including VAT.

On a line below Product L show the totals for Sales without VAT, VAT and Sales with VAT.

Save and print the spreadsheet, look carefully at the layout and make any improvements necessary. If any changes are made, print a further copy.

Part 3

Two new products are added to the range:

Product M	Cost £50.00	Number sold 6
Product N	Cost £18.50	Number sold 7

1. Add these two items and ensure that they are included in the new totals.
2. Save the spreadsheet data and print a copy of the spreadsheet.

....

TASK 5.3

Part 1

Plan and produce a spreadsheet to show the comparison of the cost of three possible venues for a concert.

The information is supplied as follows:

	Venue 1	Venue 2	Venue 3
Total costs are made up of:			
Hire of hall	10,000	8,000	6,000
Advertising	3,500	3,500	3,500
Printing	750	750	750
Total income will be made up of:			
Number of people	8,000	6,000	8,000
Cost of ticket	£2.50	£2.50	£1.50

Your display will need to show the amount of total profit or loss expected.

Save and print your spreadsheet.

Part 2

As a result of inflation, advertising has increased by 15 per cent and printing costs by £120 per venue.

Enter the changes and save and print the updated spreadsheet.

....

USING SPREADSHEETS EFFECTIVELY · SECTION 5

TASK 5.4

Part 1

A small business operates a system for calculating expenses. It has simple rules: it pays claimants 20p per mile for the first 30 miles, 15p per mile from 31 to 60 miles and then 10p per mile for journeys over 60 miles.

Mileage can be claimed once a day. There is also a subsistence allowance of breakfast £3.75, lunch £4.50 and tea £2.25.

You are required to create and produce a simple template for individual claims.

You must produce a subtotal for travel costs and a subtotal for subsistence, the total claim also needs to be calculated.

Save your template. Test your spreadsheet design with some practice data, and amend if necessary.

Part 2

The following claim is presented from Steve Tripp:

	Travel	*Subsistence*
Monday	70 miles	L
Tuesday	30 miles	none
Wednesday	200 miles	B L T
Thursday	none	none
Friday	80 miles	B L T
Saturday	10 miles	

Fill in your prepared template, making sure that you have a copy of the template for the next claimant.

Save the data for S Tripp. Print a copy of the claim.

Part 3

A claim is received from Dave Gathercole:

	Mon	Tues	Wed	Thurs	Fri	Sat
Travel	300	70	80	10	5	0
Subsistence	B L T	L	T			

Use your template to produce a printout of D Gathercole's claim. Save the data.

TASK 5.5

Part 1

Prepare a spreadsheet to show the total and average visitors to a stately home—Firwood Hall—for last August.

The information supplied is as follows:

	Week 1	*Week 2*	*Week 3*	*Week 4*
Monday	150	160	50	108
Tuesday	100	133	90	67
Wednesday	150	127	169	182
Thursday	175	130	131	156
Friday	180	200	207	193
Saturday	220	225	210	167
Sunday	270	260	290	215

You are required to provide a printout showing:

1 Total visitors for each week
2 Average weekly visitors
3 Average visitors for each day
4 Overall total visitors for August.

Part 2

The figures recorded for week 3, Monday and Tuesday, were incorrect. They should be Monday 125 visitors and Tuesday 117 visitors. Make the necessary amendments and provide an updated printout.

Part 3

The cost of visiting Firwood Hall is £1.05 Monday, Tuesday and Wednesday, £1.20 Thursday and Friday and £1.35 on Saturday and Sunday.

Make the necessary additions to the spreadsheet to show:

1 Total weekly income
2 Average weekly income
3 Total income received during August.

Produce a printout of both the spreadsheet display and contents.

....

Part 1

TASK 5.6

Create a spreadsheet to help you plan the cash forecast for the Jigsaw Company for six months. The company's managers need to consider the income and expenditure each month and be able to identify when they will have cash available or when they might need to borrow money.

They have suggested a possible layout, as follows:

```
CASH FORECAST
                    JAN   FEB   MAR   APR   MAY   JUN
INCOME
Balance b/f
Sales
Other
TOTAL INCOME

EXPENSES
Salaries
Business Rates
Rent
Materials
Others
TOTAL EXPENSES

BALANCE
```

Set up the spreadsheet and save a copy of the file.

Part 2

The company supply you with the following information to complete the spreadsheet:

- Opening balance in January was £15,000
- Sales in January £8,000; in February and March £10,000; April £25,000, May £33,000 and June £35,000
- Wages are £15,000 per month
- Rent is £1,400 per month
- Business rate is payable in February, April and June and is £2,500 per payment
- The estimated cost of materials is 30 per cent of Sales

Enter the data and check that your entries are correct. Save and print a copy of the spreadsheet.

Part 3

You are requested to present the information in the following manner:

- All numeric entries are to be in pounds and pence (£.p) format.
- The text information in the first column should be left justified and the headings in the other columns should be right justified.

Save and print a copy of the spreadsheet.

Part 4

The managers of the company want to know the effects of certain possible changes.

Present two copies of the spreadsheet. The first showing an increase in rent of 10 per cent; after printing return the rent to the original value. The second printout should show the effects of a fall of 5 per cent in material costs.

....

TASK 5.7

Part 1

Create a spreadsheet to calculate salary and commission payable to employees in a travel agent The Happy Holiday Company.

The basic salary is £200 per month. The commission payable is divided into four categories:

| Coach trips | 5 per cent | Escorted tours | 8 per cent |
| Chartered holidays | 7 per cent | Foreign hotel packages | 10 per cent |

There are six members of staff:

| G Banks | R Egan | M Nicholson |
| R Eke | C Anscott | J Lee |

Sales for each area are as follows:

- Coach trips:
  G Banks £300, R Eke £278, R Egan £44, C Anscott £127, M Nicholson £78 and J Lee £210

- Chartered Holidays:
  G Banks £150, R Eke £256, R Egan £231, C Anscott £178, M Nicholson £89 and J Lee £400

- Escorted Tours:
  G Banks £600, R Eke £158, R Egan £371, C Anscott £80,
  M Nicholson £225 and J Lee £800

- Foreign Hotel Packages:
  G Banks £356, R Eke £429, R Egan £399, C Anscott £700,
  M Nicholson £700 and J Lee £528

Complete the spreadsheet with the above data.

Part 2

You are required to amend the previous spreadsheet to take account of the following (if you have not already done so).

1. Display all numeric information to two decimal places (£.p format).

2. Generate a total for each level of commission.

3. Generate an overall total.

Save and print a copy of your spreadsheet.

Part 3

The following changes are made to the information supplied:

1. The basic salary is increased from £200 to £275.

2. All commission rates are increased by 2 per cent.

Produce a spreadsheet printout to show the effects of these changes.

....

TASK 5.8

Part 1

You are required to plan, design and create a spreadsheet to show the profit per bottle of drinks sold at the Longlands Social Club.

You are supplied with the following information:

Drink	Price per bottle/carton	Number of measures per bottle/carton
Sherry	£4.95	12
Vodka	£8.95	20
Gin	£7.90	20
Brandy	£16.00	20
Whisky	£9.89	20
Apple Juice	75p	8
Orange Juice	75p	8
Pineapple Juice	80p	8
Lemonade	85p	10

The selling price per drink, respectively, is:

60p 70p 65p 90p 65p 25p 25p 25p 20p

Calculate the cost per measure, display the selling price per drink and show the profit per measure.

Save and print a copy of the spreadsheet. Check the display and make any amendments and print an updated copy if necessary.

Part 2

The Longlands Social Club decide to sell wine:

- Red wine at £3.50 per bottle giving 8 glasses
- White wine at £2.99 per bottle giving 8 glasses
- The cost of the wine per glass will be 90p for red wine and 80p for white.

Add the two items above between whisky and apple juice.

Save the updated spreadsheet and print a copy.

Part 3

Further information is required concerning the percentage profit per bottle or carton. Create an additional column to show this information.

Part 4

Ensure that you have an appropriate main heading. Rearrange the information in alphabetical order of drink. Insert a footer with your name and today's date. Print a copy of the spreadsheet.

TASK 5.9

Part 1

Plan and create a spreadsheet to show the selling price of a range of Christmas Goods.

You are given the following information:

Product	Cost of materials (£)	Mark-up (%)
Xmas crackers	4.99	200
Xmas cards	2.99	100
Xmas decorations	3.99	250
Calendars	4.50	300
Serviettes	1.75	200
Tablecloths	3.75	150
Candles	1.25	175

You are required to show two further columns, the amount of the mark-up and then the selling price.

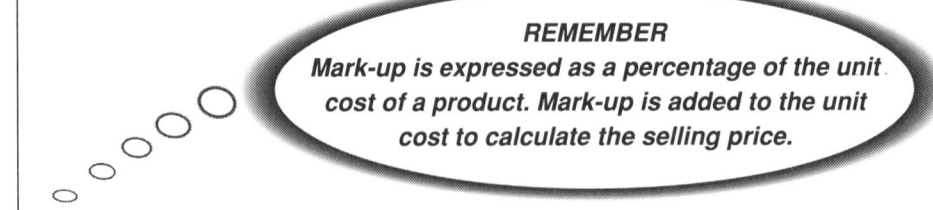

> **REMEMBER**
> Mark-up is expressed as a percentage of the unit cost of a product. Mark-up is added to the unit cost to calculate the selling price.

Display the information in £.p format. Save and print a copy of the spreadsheet display and contents.

Part 2

Sort the information in your spreadsheet in ascending order of value of percentage mark-up.

Calculate and display the average percentage mark-up on the goods sold.

SECTION 5 · USING SPREADSHEETS EFFECTIVELY

Part 3

The following changes are to be made:

1 The cost of Xmas crackers increases by 10 per cent.

2 The percentage mark-up on candles increases by 25 per cent.

3 Add candle holders at £5.99 with a mark-up of 180 per cent.

Rearrange the information in alphabetical order of product. Save and print a copy of the spreadsheet information. Make a copy of the data and back the data onto a second disk.

....

Part 1

TASK 5.10

You are supplied with the following information:

1 To calculate the area of a room, multiply its length by its width.
Example: If a room is 3 metres long and 2 metres wide then area equals 3m × 2m which equals 6 square metres.

2 The room dimensions are as follows:

Bedroom 1	7m × 5m	Kitchen	4m × 5m
Bedroom 2	6m × 5m	Dining room	5m × 5m
Bedroom 3	5m × 5m	Utility room	3m × 2m
Bedroom 4	4m × 6m	Playroom	4m × 4m
Living room	8m × 5m		

3 The bedrooms are to be carpeted in lightweight cord
The living room in twist pile
The dining room in all wool Axminster
The utility room and kitchen in kitchen flooring
The playroom in heavy duty cord.

EASY CARPET WAREHOUSE		
Carpet	Cost per square metre	Cost including laying
Lightweight cord	£4.95	£5.60
Heavy duty cord	£6.60	£7.15
Twist pile	£7.25	£8.10
All wool Axminster	£9.60	£10.25
Kitchen flooring	£3.99	£5.20

You are required to create a spreadsheet, showing the carpeting requirements for each room together with the price—including and excluding laying—in accordance with the Easy Carpet Warehouse's advertising leaflet.

The suggested labels for column 1 are:

Length in metres
Width in metres
Area in square metres
Cost per square metre, including laying
Total cost, including laying
Cost per square metre, excluding laying
Total cost, excluding laying

Show both room and carpet type in the columns across the spreadsheet.

Save the data and print a copy of the spreadsheet.

Part 2

Recall the file of information from Part 1.

Add three more rows to your spreadsheet. Carry the figures for 'Total cost for carpet and laying' and 'Total cost for carpet only' and in the final row show the savings that could be made if you laid the carpets yourself.

Part 3

Imagine there is a price rise of 10 per cent on all carpets and that fitting costs increase by the 10 per cent plus £1.50. What will be the total increase in price to fit carpets in all the rooms in the house?

Part 4

Using the same information, produce a similar spreadsheet for your own house.

FURTHER SPREADSHEET ACTIONS AND FUNCTIONS: II

SECTION 6

....

This section explores some further functions and facilities that may be available to you once you are familiar with basic spreadsheet actions.

....

6.1 PRODUCING INFORMATION IN GRAPHIC FORMAT

With some packages the numeric information stored in a spreadsheet can be presented in diagrammatic or graphic format. The charts and graphs that result will show the relationship between numbers in a pictorial form and often provide an easier way of communicating information.

Several types of graph are commonly used.

Bar graph or chart

This form of graph uses bars or columns of the same width. The length or height of the bar is related to the number of items in each category. This format is used to make comparison over time between items; for example, it could show expenses over a year, month by month. The display of the pictorial information can be presented vertically (Fig. 6.1a) or horizontally (Fig. 6.1b).

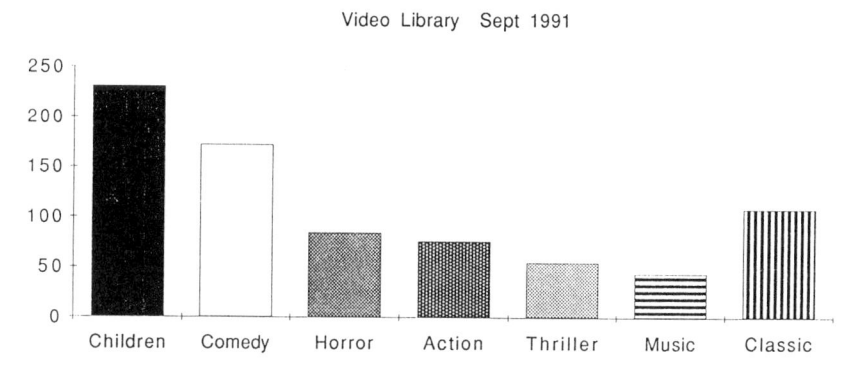

Figure 6.1a Vertical bar graph

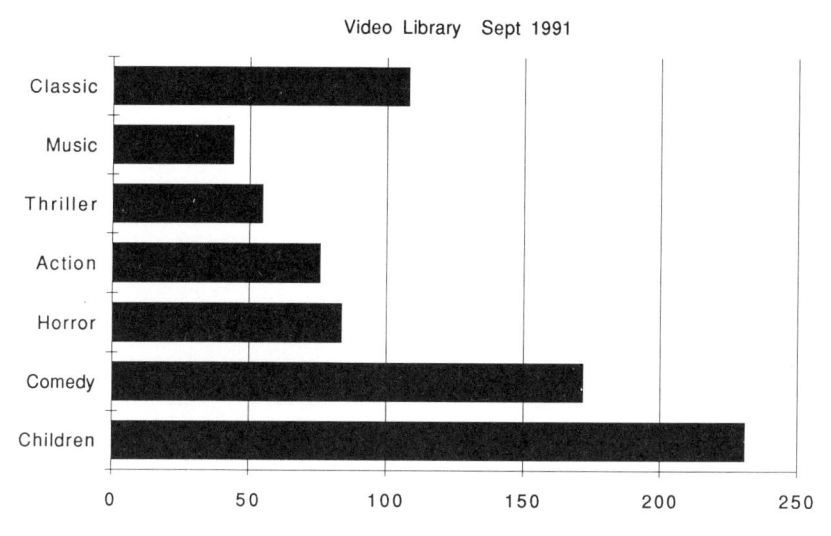

Figure 6.1b Horizontal bar graph

USING SPREADSHEETS EFFECTIVELY • SECTION 6

Histogram

This is a special kind of block graph. The main difference in a histogram is that the frequency is governed by the **area** of the column rather than the height. The widths of individual blocks or bars may vary.

Line graph

A line graph (Fig. 6.2) is formed where a number of points that are identified by using the information supplied on axis* are joined together to create a line. This type of graph provides a useful display for conversion tables or for showing changes in values over a period of time.

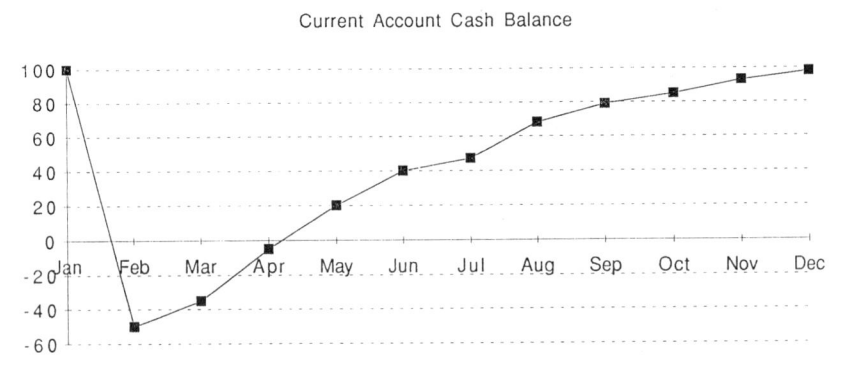

Figure 6.2 Line graph

The graph may contain a single line or multiple lines.

Pie charts

A pie chart is a circle that is divided into sectors or wedges like slices of a cake or pie. As each sector represents a fraction of the whole circle, it is therefore a useful method of showing each sector's contribution to the whole. For example, the following information can be displayed in a pie chart.

No. of children	Favourite food
10	Chips
5	Pizza
7	Beans
8	Hamburger

The pie chart could be displayed as a complete circle (Fig. 6.3a), or segments could be separated from the main circle, which is sometimes referred to as an 'exploded wedge' (Fig. 6.3b).

---

*An axis is a line that is used to define a scale and serves as a major reference for plotting data on a chart. The horizontal axis is referred to as the x axis and the vertical axis is referred to as the y axis.

Children's Favourite Foods

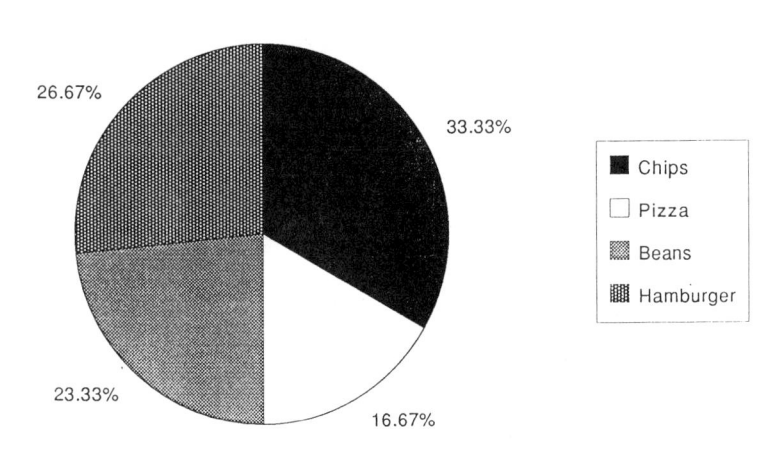

26.67%

33.33%

■ Chips
□ Pizza
▨ Beans
▦ Hamburger

23.33%

16.67%

Figure 6.3a   Pie chart

Children's Favourite Foods

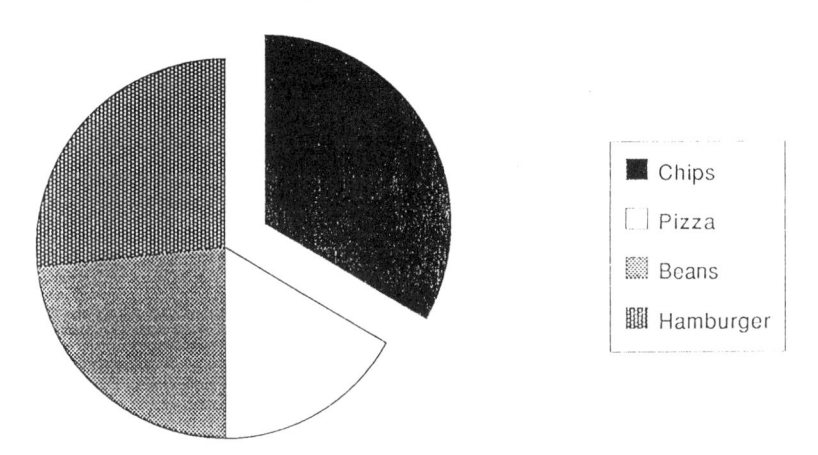

■ Chips
□ Pizza
▨ Beans
▦ Hamburger

Figure 6.3b   'Exploded' pie chart

Scatter diagram

This form of graph can be used to show the relationship between two measurements for each item of data. For example, if you collected information about height and weight of a number of people (Fig. 6.4a), a scatter diagram would allow you to see if the taller people were heavier (Fig. 6.4b). It is a useful form of graph for finding patterns or trends (see Fig. 6.4c).

	A	B	C
1	HEIGHTS AND WEIGHTS OF 10 MEN		
2			
3	HEIGHT cm	WEIGHT kg	
4	168	65	
5	178	77	
6	183	78	
7	158	58	
8	162	63	
9	189	82	
10	152	57	
11	191	86	
12	172	69	
13	175	74	

Figure 6.4a   Spreadsheet of heights and weights of a group

USING SPREADSHEETS EFFECTIVELY • SECTION 6

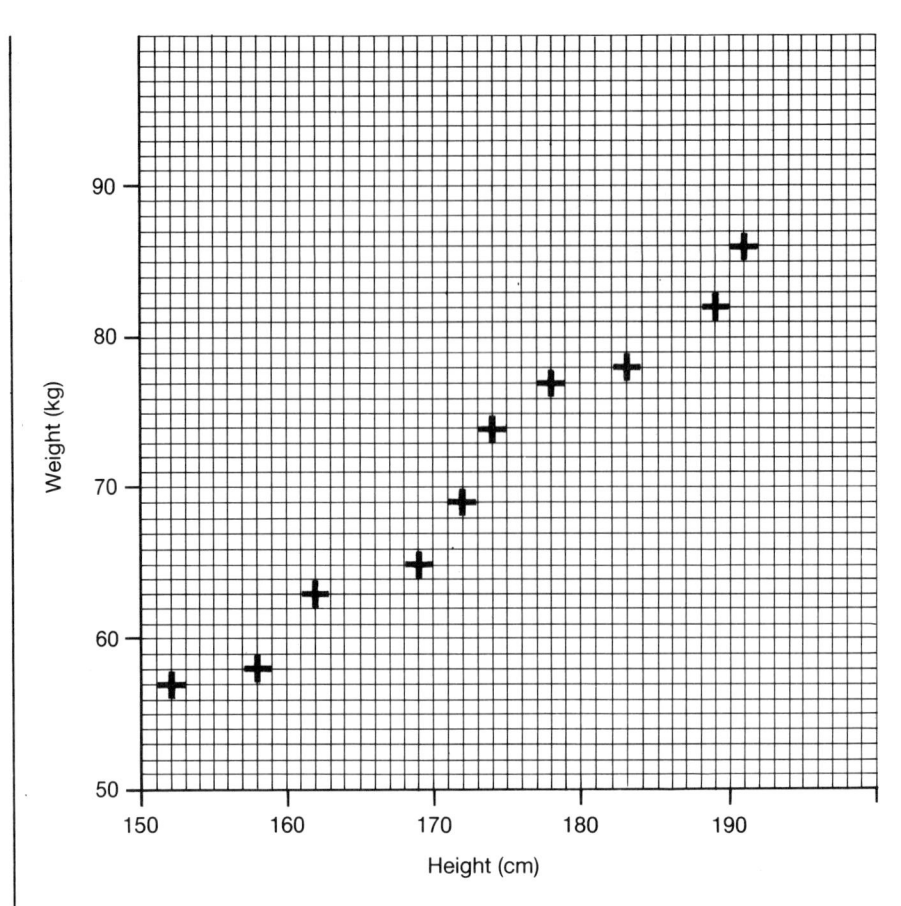

Figure 6.4b Scattergram showing heights and weights of the group

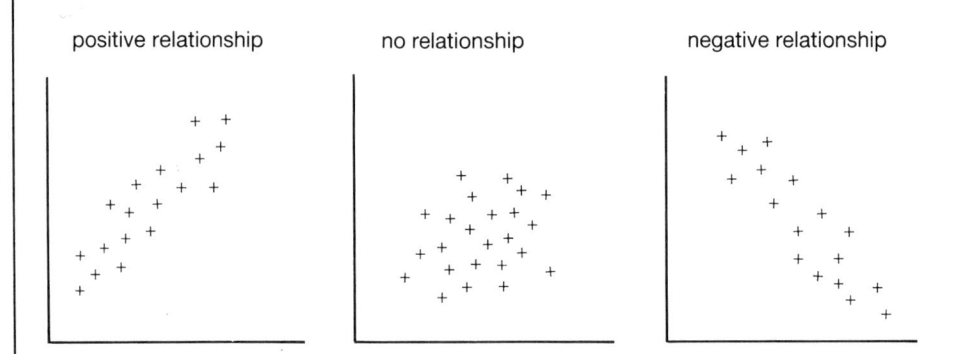

Figure 6.4c Scattergram showing relationship trends

Stacked charts

This is a form of bar graph that 'stacks' information. It is useful for showing how a 'total' is built up (see Fig. 6.5).

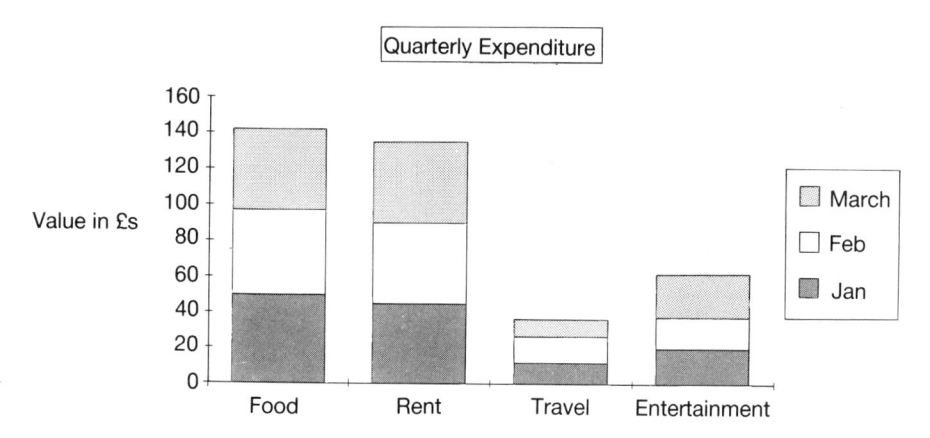

Figure 6.5 Stacked bar chart of quarterly expenditure

Grouped bar chart

This is a method of presenting a bar chart with information grouped together for easier interpretation (see Figs 6.6a and 6.6b). A grouped bar chart could be a simple bar chart or a stacked bar chart.

	A		C	D
1	Expenditure			
2		Jan	Feb	March
3	Food	50	47	45
4	Rent	45	45	45
5	Travel	12	15	10
6	Entertainment	20	18	25

Data for stacked and grouped bar chart.

Figure 6.6a Spreadsheet of grouped bar chart shown in Fig. 6.6b and stacked bar chart in Fig. 6.5

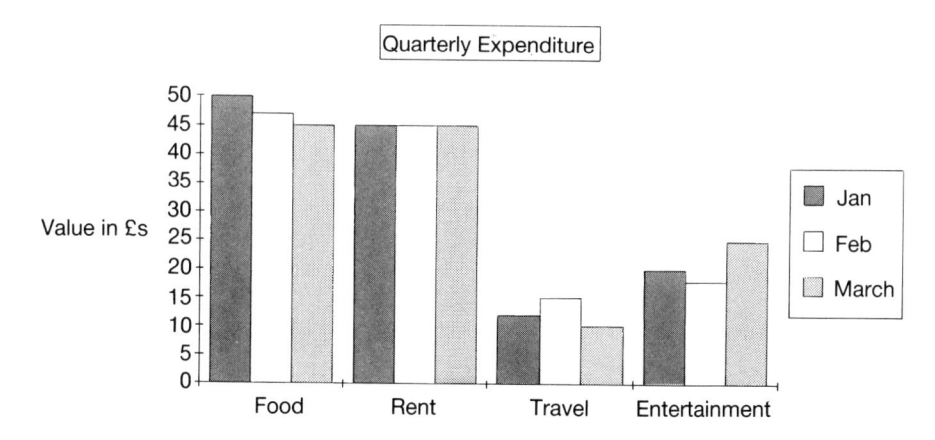

Figure 6.6b Grouped bar chart of quarterly expenditure

USING SPREADSHEETS EFFECTIVELY • **SECTION 6**

Picture graph or pictogram

This graph, shown in Fig. 6.7, uses symbols instead of bars or lines.

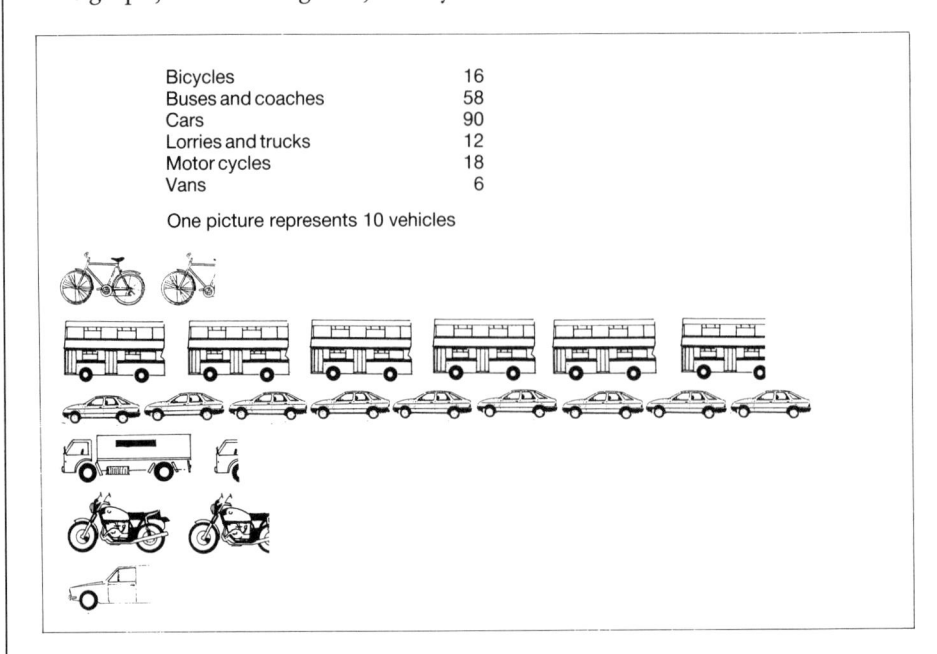

Bicycles	16
Buses and coaches	58
Cars	90
Lorries and trucks	12
Motor cycles	18
Vans	6

One picture represents 10 vehicles

Figure 6.7 Picture graph

Combined graphs

It is possible to have a combination of a line graph and a bar graph (as in Fig. 6.8). However, whichever form of graph is used, it is essential to provide information in order for the graphs to be correctly interpreted (see Fig. 6.9). Such information should include:

- a title
- axis clearly labelled and the scale shown for all graphs
- sectors/wedges labelled for pie charts
- an explanation of any codes used.

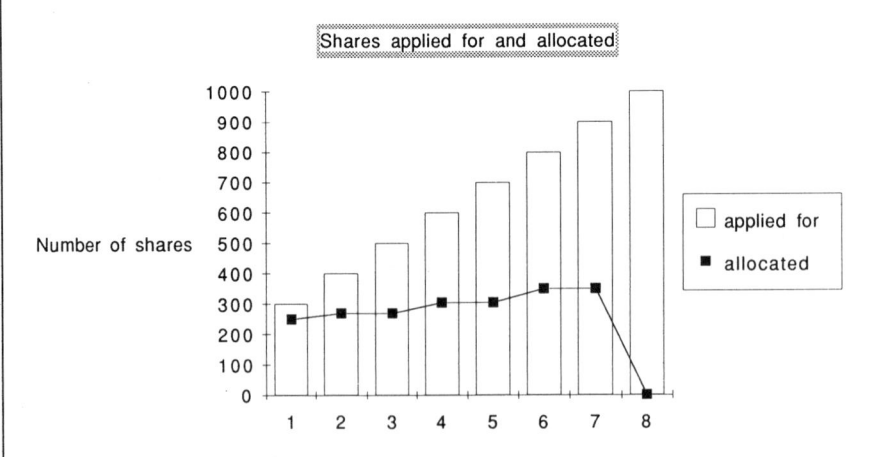

Figure 6.8 Combined line and bar graph

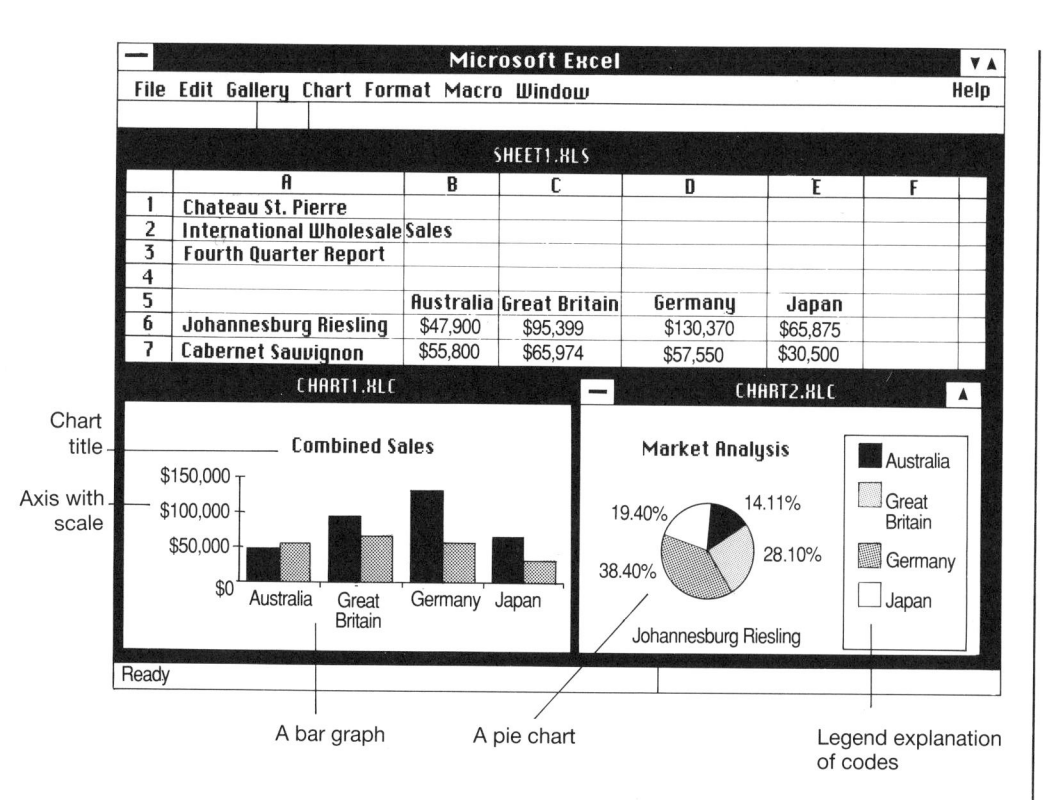

Figure 6.9 Excel screen showing two charts created from spreadsheet data

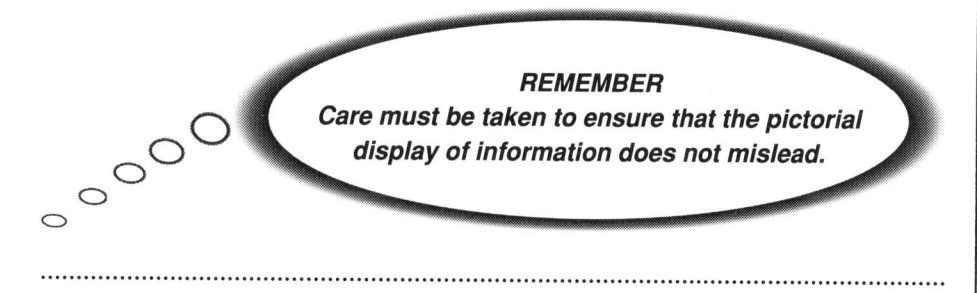

> **REMEMBER**
> *Care must be taken to ensure that the pictorial display of information does not mislead.*

This is a facility offered by some packages for automating routine tasks to a single instruction. It is a system of programming your spreadsheet to carry out complex tasks in the least amount of time with the greatest accuracy.

To operate a macro you need to:

- give the macro a name
- carry out the sequence of actions
- save that sequence of actions.

You can then recall the macro when you require the same routine to be carried out.

You would be well advised to produce documentation to support any macros you create. The exact system of operation will vary with each package.

6.2 CREATING MACROS

6.3 NAMING SPREADSHEET CELLS OR CELL RANGES

This facility is particularly useful when constructing formulas. It will allow you to name an individual cell or range of cells, and you simply use that name in your formula instead of a cell reference, as shown in Fig. 6.10.

	A	B	C
1	VAT rate	17.5%	
2			
3	PRODUCT	PRICE	PRICE incl. VAT
4	Videos	3.99	= VATrate * B3
5	Cassettes	1.99	= VATrate * B4

B1 name is VATrate

Figure 6.10 Naming an individual cell (or cells)

6.4 HIDING CELL CONTENTS

It may be that your spreadsheet contains sensitive information, e.g. salaries. You may decide that you do not want to display this information on a screen yet you require the data as part of the spreadsheet. If so, you may be able to hide the contents of individual cells or rows and columns. This will also offer a system of protecting information from accidental or unauthorized changes.

6.5 FREEZING OR FIXING WORKSHEET TITLES, ETC.

This facility is particularly useful when you are operating a large spreadsheet and the descriptive information scrolls off the screen. You can hold or fix certain information on the screen and the remainder of the information scrolls as before. In Fig. 6.11, row 1, which contains the headings, has been frozen, as have columns A and B which contain the product name and catalogue number.

	A	B	K	L	M	N	O
1							
17							
18							
19							
20							
21							
22							

Row 1 remains fixed

This part of the spreadsheet scrolls

Columns A and B remain fixed

This part of the spreadsheet scrolls

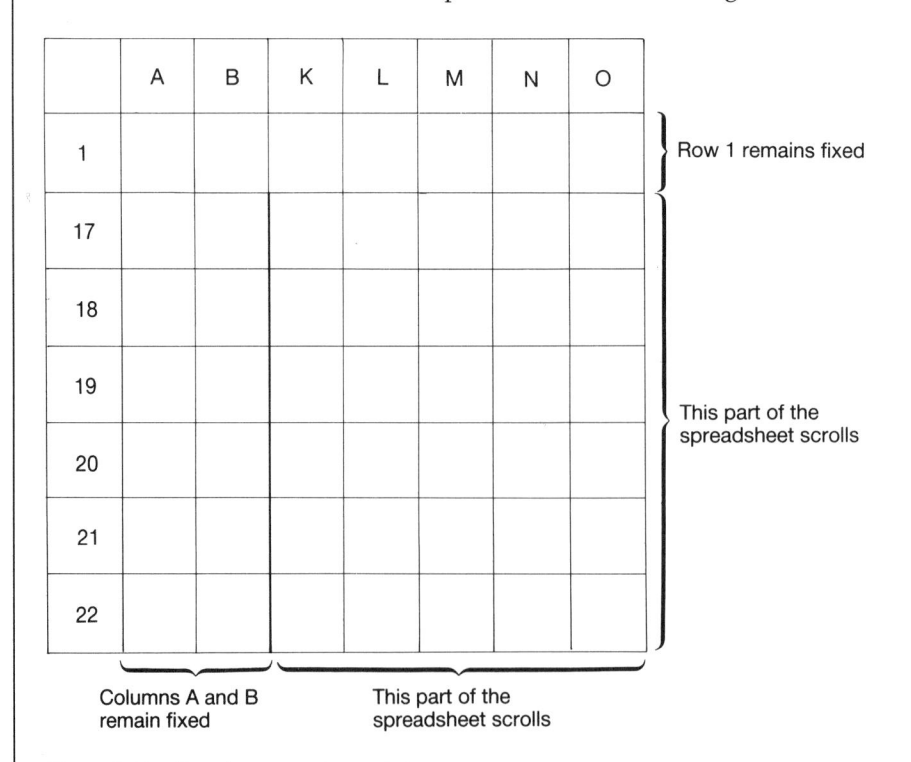

Figure 6.11 Freezing parts of a worksheet

6.6 CONDITIONS AND LOOK-UP FUNCTIONS

When using the IF function and an operator such as:

- = equal to
- < less than
- \> greater than
- < > not equal to

you can provide a display of information if the specified circumstances hold.

For example, if you were preparing a spreadsheet for a business that offered a discount of 10 per cent for quantities sold of over 20, then you could complete the spreadsheet as in Fig. 6.12.

	A	B	C
1	PRICE	25.00	20.00
2	Number sold	30	10
3	Price charged		

Figure 6.12 Preparing a spreadsheet with specified conditions

In cell B3 would be:

IF(B2>20, B1*.9*B2, B1*B4)

which in effect means that if the number sold, i.e. B2, is greater than 20 then multiply the price by .9 (to find the price less 10 per cent discount) then multiply by the number sold. If the number sold is not greater than 20 then multiply the price by the number sold.

This would result in a value of £675 in B2 and if the function was replicated to C3 then this would result in a value of £200.

The **look-up** feature enables you to use data entered on the spreadsheet as reference/source data. The information you require to use the look-up function is:

- the cell to hold the result
- the cells to use for the source data
- the cells that store the information resulting from the source data.

	A	B	C	D
1	Code	Price		
2	K	21		
3	L	22		
4	M	23		
5	N	24		
6	O	25		
7				
8	Name	No. bought	Code	Cost
9	P Jones	10	L	
10	E Davies	5	O	

Figure 6.13 Using the look-up function

For example, in Fig. 6.13, the function in D9 could be:

LOOKUP(C9, A2..A6, B2..B6)*B9

The effect of this function is that the cost will be placed in D9. To calculate the cost the code stored in C9 is compared with the list stored in the range of A2..A6. If that value is found, then the corresponding figure in the range B2..B6 is taken, and in this situation is multiplied by the number of items sold, i.e. the value stored in B9. The resulting value in D9 would be £2.20 (22p × 10). If the function was replicated to D10, the result would be £1.25 (25p × 5).

6.7 ADDITIONAL FUNCTIONS

You have probably already considered some functions, such as SUM, AVE, MIN, MAX, which were introduced on page 12.

Your handbook will provide you with a complete list of those available to you when using your system.

Some others you might like to consider are:

- Search for a particular item of text
- Replace one item of text for another
- Enter today's date
- Enter the current time
- Calculate depreciation of a value
- Calculate future value of an investment or loan
- Calculate interest payments for an investment or loan over a given period
- Calculate net present value
- Calculate standard deviation
- Display absolute values—i.e. return a positive value whether the number stored is negative or positive
- Display integer values—i.e. the whole number value only
- Display rounded values—i.e. the value rounded up or down to the nearest whole number
- Calculation of cosine of a number

- Calculation of sine of a number
- Calculation of tangent of a number.

6.8 INTEGRATING YOUR SPREADSHEET WITH OTHER SOFTWARE APPLICATIONS

It may be possible to use your spreadsheet as a word processor or database, or in combination with other packages. Such facilities are usually fairly limited, but are available commercially.

You may also wish to investigate ways in which you can import and export your spreadsheet files to other computer applications such as word processing and desk-top publishing.

6.9 CHECKLIST

Areas covered in Section 6

You should have considered the purpose of and how to perform:

1. Producing information graphic format using:
   - line graphs
   - block or column graphs
   - histograms
   - pie charts
   - stacked block graphs
   - scattergrams
   - combination graphs.

2. Creating and using spreadsheet macros.

3. Naming spreadsheet cells or cell ranges.

4. Hiding information in cells, rows or columns.

5. Fixing or freezing spreadsheet titles and/or column/row headings.

6. Using IF and LOOKUP functions.

7. Additional functions offered by your system.

8. Linking your spreadsheet with other computer application packages.

9. Using other computer application facilities within your spreadsheet.

SECTION 7

ACTIVITIES

This section contains a variety of activities you might wish to try to solve using a spreadsheet.

TASK 7.1

Provide a conversion table for temperatures on the Fahrenheit and Celsius scales.

The range of temperatures to be covered is from 0 degrees to 100 degrees on Celsius at 1 degree intervals.

The formulas you require are:

- To convert C to F, multiply C by 9 divided by 5 and add 32.
- To convert F to C, subtract 32 from F and multiply by 5 divided by 9.

Save and print a copy of the spreadsheet.
Plot the information on a line graph.

TASK 7.2

Provide two conversion tables for litres to gallons and gallons to litres.

The range of gallons to be covered is from 1 to 8. The range of litres is from 1 to 25.

The conversion rate is:

- To convert gallons to litres, multiply by 4.54.
- To convert litres to gallons, multiply by 0.22.

TASK 7.3

Provide a conversion range similar to Task 7.2 but for feet and metres. Select suitable ranges.

The conversion is calculated as follows:

- To convert feet to metres, multiply by 0.3048.
- To convert metres to feet, multiply by 3.28.

TASK 7.4

Part 1

Using a source book, collect data on population for ten items for either countries in the EC or areas of the UK for three time periods, e.g. 1970, 1980 and 1990.

Create and set up a spreadsheet to hold the information. Save the data and produce a printout of the information in graphic format; include suitable headings, etc.

Part 2

Show the total for each time period selected. Calculate the percentage contribution of each counry or area for each time period. Create additional columns where appropriate to display the information.

Save the amended information and print a copy of the spreadsheet and graphs to show the percentages calculated.

Part 1

TASK 7.5

Create a spreadsheet to show the exchange values for £10, £50, £100, £500 and £1,000.

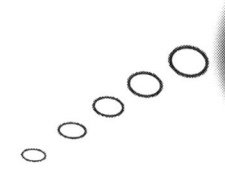

> **REMEMBER**
> To change pounds sterling into foreign currency X: multiply the amount in pounds sterling by the number of X in one pound sterling. To change currency X into pounds sterling: first divide the total amount of X by the number of X in one pound sterling and then round your answer to the nearest penny.

In this exercise, use the following exchange rates:

Country	Currency	£1 buys
Australia	Dollars	2.4050
Austria	Schillings	19.75
Belgium	Francs	58.25
Canada	Dollars	2.17
Denmark	Kroner	10.95
Holland	Guilders	3.19
Finland	Marks	6.9
France	Francs	9.6
Germany	Marks	2.82
Greece	Drachma	299
Hong Kong	Dollars	14.5
Ireland	Punts	1.065
Italy	Lira	2145
Japan	Yen	255
Malta	Pounds	0.562
New Zealand	Dollars	3.17
Norway	Kroner	11.13
Portugal	Escudos	252
Spain	Pesetas	179.5
Sweden	Kronor	10.76
Switzerland	Francs	2.407
Turkey	Lira	5400
United States	Dollars	1.8675

Save your spreadsheet data. Print a copy of your spreadsheet.

Part 2

Use the spreadsheet created in Part 1, but this time use the current exchange values. This information is generally available in newspapers or from high street banks.

....

USING SPREADSHEETS EFFECTIVELY • SECTION 7

TASK 7.6

Part 1

Plan and produce a spreadsheet to show the net and gross pay for each member of staff and the total gross and net pay of the Alphabet Company.

You are given the following information:

> Basic wage rate is £5 per hour
> Overtime wage rate is £6 per hour
> Tax rate is 0.25 (i.e. tax payable is at 25p in £1)

The members of staff and the hours worked are:

	Basic hours	Overtime hours
Sewell J	20	3
Ireson E	20	2
Cross J	30	0
Drew D	10	0
Evans M	20	5
Jones M	25	2
Balfour K	20	8
Grover S	30	6.5
Holland P	25	3.5
Kavanagh M	32	4
James D	27	1.5
David J	27	1.5

The following formulas are provided:

> Gross pay = (Basic hours worked × Basic rate) + (Overtime hours worked × Overtime rate)
> Tax payable = Gross pay × Tax rate
> Net pay = Gross pay − Tax payable

Part 2

After you note the answers/results to each part of the question below, return to the spreadsheet information at the end of Part 1.

(a) What is the increase to gross pay and net pay of a 10 per cent increase in the basic wage rate and 8.75 per cent increase in the overtime wage rate?
(b) How much would be payable to D James if he worked 30 hours basic and 4.5 hours overtime?
(c) What would be the difference in the total net pay if the tax rate increases to 27 per cent and then 30 per cent?
(d) What would be the total net wage bill if tax was 35 per cent, the basic rate of pay was £5.65 and the overtime rate was £6.85?

TASK 7.7

You require a catalogue of garden plants to complete this task or you could adapt the task to use with any sales catalogue.

Imagine you own a small gardening and landscaping business and you have been asked to provide plants for a local park.

You have £1,000 to spend. The park committee only want 10 varieties of flowers. Use a spreadsheet to find out how many of each you can order for the money available.

The column headings suggested are:

Plant name   Cat. no.   Cost per unit   No. required   Cost

VAT at 17.5%   Total

You will also have to include a fixed planting charge of £200, payable only once, to which VAT needs to be added.

Aim to make the cost of your plant selection as near to £1,000 as possible. On your spreadsheet show totals for cost of plants and planting charge, VAT payable, and cost of plants and planting charge plus VAT.

TASK 7.8

Part 1

Using the spreadsheet information provided, create a spreadsheet as shown to calculate price changes with a given inflation rate. Insert a suitable heading and adjust any formulas necessary.

Spreadsheet contents:

	A	B	C
1	PRICE £		200
2	INFLATION %		10
3	INFLATION FACTOR		(C2+100)/100
4			
5			
6	YEAR	PRICE	
7	1985	C1*C3	
8	A7+1	B7*C3	
9	A8+1	B8*C3	
10	A9+1	B9*C3	

Replicate down from A8 and B8 as necessary.

Note: Entries in C3, A8, A9, A10, B7, B8, B9 and B10 are formulas.
Entries in A1, A2, A3, A6 and B6 are text or labels.
Entries in C1, C2 and C7 are numeric entries.

Part 2

Explain the formulas used in cells C3, A8, B7 and B8.

Part 3

Use the spreadsheet created to show the effects of the following situations:

1	Price £50	Inflation 12 per cent	Base year 1987	Value in 1994
2	Price £200	Inflation 10 per cent	Base year 1965	Value in 1989
3	Price £350	Inflation 8.5 per cent	Base year 1985	Value in 2010

TASK 7.9

Part 1

The following weather data are for the first week in January:

Date	Minimum temp.	Maximum temp.	Rainfall (mm)
1	−2	5	1
2	−3	6	0
3	0	3	0
4	1	5	2.5
5	−4	2	1.5
6	−3	1	0
7	2	3	0

Design a spreadsheet layout to store the above information. The spreadsheet should show:

- average weekly minimum temperature
- average weekly maximum temperature
- average weekly rainfall.

Display the highest minimum temperature and the highest maximum temperature; the lowest minimum temperature and the lowest maximum temperature; and the highest and lowest rainfall.

Part 2

Adapt the design to take the data for a calendar month. Test your design with sample data.

Part 3

1. Design a similar spreadsheet template to hold the data for one year's weather.
2. Display the average monthly maximum and minimum temperatures and rainfall.
3. Display the total monthly and annual rainfall.
4. Test your design with sample data and amend if necessary.

TASK 7.10

Design spreadsheet templates to perform the following activities. Test your designs with sample data.

1. Design a spreadsheet to maintain the balance on a current account for a bank or building society. Show income and expenditure and the balance of the account after each transaction.

2. Design a spreadsheet to show the value of a portfolio of stocks and shares at current prices. The spreadsheet could be extended to calculate yield on stocks and shares.

3. Design a spreadsheet to present the results of an election. Show clearly the percentage vote for each candidate.

4. Design a spreadsheet to calculate mortgage repayments for a sum of money, over a stated period of time, at a specified interest rate.

5. Design a spreadsheet to calculate depreciation of an asset.

SECTION 7 · USING SPREADSHEETS EFFECTIVELY

Fun with numbers

TASK 7.11

Try out or solve the following puzzles using spreadsheet facilities.

1. The number 142857 has six digits. Multiply this number by 2, 3, 4 and so on. What do you notice about the result? Can you find any other numbers that produce a similar result?

2. Using all the numbers 0, 1, 2, 3, 4, 5, 6, 7, 8 and 9 create formulas that add up to exactly 100. For example:

$$1 + 2 + 3 + 4 + 5 + 6 + 7 + (8 \times 9) = 100$$

3. Think of a number.
   Add 3 to the number.
   Now double it.
   Subtract 4.
   Halve it.
   Subtract the number you first thought of.

   What will the answer always be? Will it work for negative numbers as well as positive ones?

4. Think of a number that is less than 5. Add 5. Double this. Subtract 10. Divide by 2.

   Try this with all numbers under 5. What do you notice about the answers? Will this work with numbers over 5?

5. Numbers form patterns. Below are some examples:

$$(1 \times 8) + 1 = 9$$
$$(12 \times 8) + 2 = 98$$
$$(123 \times 8) + 3 = 987$$
$$(1234 \times 8) + 4 = 9876$$
$$(12345 \times 8) + 5 = 98765$$

$$(1 \times 9) + 2 = 11$$
$$(12 \times 9) + 3 = 111$$
$$(123 \times 9) + 4 = 1111$$
$$(1234 \times 9) + 5 = 11111$$

Can you find any other patterns?

6. Test this *number nine* trick.

   Add the digits of any numbers and subtract them from the original number. The number will always be 9 or divisible by 9. For example:

   (a) Take the number 783.
   (b) Add the digits 7 + 8 + 3 = 18.
   (c) Subtract the second number from the first: 783 − 18 = 765.

   If the answer is not 9 then it can be divided by 9: 765/9 = 85.

7   *Magic squares*   In a magic square, all the numbers in the square are placed in such an arrangement that each column, or row or diagonal adds up to the same total. For example:

4	9	2	(= 15)
3	5	7	(= 15)
8	1	6	(= 15)

(= 15) (= 15) (= 15)   (= 15) [diagonal]

Can you complete the following squares?

16	2	3	
5		10	8
9	7		12
	14	15	1

8		6
4		2

Can you create a magic square using the numbers 1 to 25, where the total in every direction is 65?

8   *Fibonacci series*   In the Middle Ages an Italian mathematician discovered a sequence of numbers that is built up as follows:

Start with 0 and 1
Add 0 and 1 = 1
Add 1 and 1 = 2
Add the last two results together   1 + 2 = 3
Add the last two results together   2 + 3 = 5
Add the last two results together   3 + 5 = 8

Continue the sequence until you reach 233 as a result.

Now try these:

Choose any three numbers that follow each other, e.g. 2, 3, 5
Square the middle number
Multiply the first and third numbers
Subtract the two numbers
The result should always be 1.

Take any four numbers that follow each other, e.g. 3, 5, 8, 13
Multiply the outside numbers
Multiply the inside numbers
Subtract the outside numbers from the inside numbers
The result should always be 1.

Discover more about this number series and test the results using a spreadsheet.

SECTION 7 • USING SPREADSHEETS EFFECTIVELY

9 *Triangular numbers*   These are calculated as follows:

Triangular number	Calculation	Result
1st	1	1
2nd	1 + 2	3
3rd	1 + 2 + 3	6
4th	1 + 2 + 3 + 4	10

Calculate the 5th, 6th, 7th, 8th, 9th and 10th triangular numbers.

Investigate the statement that every whole number is the sum of two or three triangular numbers; for example,

$$2 = 1 + 1$$
$$9 = 3 + 6$$
$$10 = 6 + 3 + 1$$
$$8 = 6 + 1 + 1$$

Which triangular numbers add up to 16, 29 and 48?

GLOSSARY OF TERMS

Absolute cell reference (compare and contrast *Relative cell reference*)
A cell reference that, when used in a formula, will always refer to the original cell regardless of where the formula is copied.

Active cell
The cell where information is about to be entered or edited. It indicates the user's position on the spreadsheet.

Address
A combination of row and column reference that identifies a particular cell, e.g. B2 (i.e. column B, row 2) or R2C2 (i.e. row 2, column 2).

Alignment (see also *Format*)
A reference to the method of display of information, e.g. text can be right aligned, left aligned or centred. Numbers can also be aligned as selected, though in normal practice numbers are aligned at the left.

Axis
The horizontal or vertical line used on a graph to indicate a value.

Block graph
A graph where the information is represented in columns or bars measured against axis. The length of the bar is related to the number of times something happened or was measured.

Cell
A single cell or box on a spreadsheet grid. A cell can store a number, text or a formula.

Cell reference
A means of referring to a particular cell on a spreadsheet. The cell will be identified by reference to the row and the column.

Circular reference
A cell entry that depends on itself to calculate a result, e.g. if the formula stored in cell A1 was A3/A1*8.

Column
A line of cells down a spreadsheet grid.

Column width
The number of characters that can be stored in a column.

Contents (compare with *Display*)
The information stored in each cell. For example, if the contents of a cell are 7+5, then the display is 12.

Cursor
A marker or highlight box that indicates the user's position on the spreadsheet.

Database
An organized set of information that is stored in a computer system. The information can be retrieved, updated, extended, sorted and searched.

Default value
The setting or display feature a spreadsheet assumes unless it is changed. For example, the column width for all columns may be 10 characters; the text will be displayed left justified.

Directory
A list of files stored on a disk.

Disk
A storage medium for data and programs. There are several types of disk, e.g. floppy disk, hard disk.

Displayed (displayed values) (compare with *Contents* and *Stored values*)
The information that results from the contents of a cell. For example, if the contents of a cell are 7+5, then the display is 12.

Edit
The process of making changes or corrections to an entry or an existing spreadsheet layout.

File name
The name that is given to the data stored on a disk.

Fonts
A set of characters in a specified format. For example, roman, italic, bold of various designs.

Times	**Univers**	**Rockwell**
Times	*Univers*	*Rockwell*
Times	Univers	Rockwell

Footer (compare with *Header*)
A line or lines of information printed below the spreadsheet grid. The type of information normally contained is the page number, date, and name of the person preparing the spreadsheet.

Format
Layout and design of document on screen or paper.

Formula
An expression of a relationship between numbers that performs a calculation. Formulas contain numbers, variables and arithmetical or mathematical functions. The following common signs are used: + (plus), − (minus), * (multiplication), / (divide). Examples of formula are:

A1 + A2 + A3   B13/100   (G1−H5)*13

Functions
An instruction to carry out a particular process. Each function has a name. If you need to carry out the function you simply use the name recognized by your

spreadsheet. A function could be described as a pre-recorded formula. For example, if you need to add together a long column of figures you could use the formula

$$A1+A2+A3+A4+A5+A6$$

or you might be able to use the function SUM, e.g. SUM(A1..A6).

Global (compare with *Range*)
A reference to an action that will affect all the cells on a spreadsheet.

Graph
A representation of numeric data in a graphic format. Main types of graphs are: line graphs, pie charts, histograms, block graphs and scatter graphs.

Grid lines
The horizontal and vertical lines on a spreadsheet or graph.

Header (compare with *Footer*)
A line or lines of information printed at the top of each page of a spreadsheet. The type of information contained is normally the file name, page number, name of business or any other specified information.

Hidden cells
Cells that can contain information but, unless referenced by a special command, will not be shown on the screen.

Histogram
A form of bar graph where the area of the bar or column represents the number of times something happened or was measured.

Integer value
A whole number display of the value stored in a spreadsheet. Integers can be positive or negative. For example 10, −2, 200 are integers 2.2, −3.708 are not. If a value of 17.66 was entered in a cell, then the integer display would be 17.

Label
A series of characters—which could include figures—that are to be treated as text, i.e. they cannot be used in a formula or calculation.

Line graphs
A graph where points are plotted using information on the horizontal and vertical axes. The points are then joined up to form a line.

Locked cells
A reference to cells where the contents cannot be changed without first 'unlocking' the cell. It provides a form of security of data as it makes it more difficult to alter data accidentally.

Macro
A system for automating routine tasks to a single instruction.

Menu
A list of items or options presented for selection.

Page break
An instruction to print the work that follows immediately on a new page.

Pie chart
A graphic diagram that is used to compare data. A circle is divided into portions or slices, each slice representing a fraction of the whole circle.

Protected cell
A system for ensuring that the contents of individual cells or cell ranges cannot be changed accidentally without a clear instruction.

Range
A system of identification of part of a spreadsheet: a particular row or column or part of a particular row or column. For example, B2..B7 will represent the values stored in B2, B3, B4, B5, B6 and B7.

Relative cell reference
A cell reference that, when used in a replicated formula, will change relative to its new position.

Replicate
A facility offered on spreadsheets, allowing the contents of cells to be copied from one part of the sheet to another.

Row
A line of cells across a spreadsheet grid.

Spreadsheet (see also *Worksheet*)
An electronic means of storing information in a computer system. The spreadsheet is composed of cells organized in rows and columns.

Status line/area
A display of information on the screen, giving information on the current or active cell, current or active cell contents, amount of space free, etc.

Stored values (compare and contrast with *Displayed values*)
A reference to the values inserted in a spreadsheet. These may differ from the displayed values. For example, if 35.67 is entered in a spreadsheet and it is displayed to one decimal place, then the stored value is 35.67 but the displayed value is 35.7.

Template
A structured spreadsheet that already contains formula and formatting instructions and is ready to be used with data.

Title
The text that is used as a heading for a spreadsheet, column/row or graph.

Value
A number or formula entry on a spreadsheet.

Worksheet (see also *Spreadsheet*)
An electronic means of storing information in a computer system. The worksheet is composed of cells organized in rows and columns.

INDEX

Absolute cell reference, 23–24, 62
Active cell, 6, 62
Address, 1, 62
Alignment, 62
Axis, 62

Bar graphs, 43–47, 62
   grouped, 47
   stacked, 46–47

Cell, 1, 7, 11, 62
Cell reference, 1–2, 62
Circular reference, 62
Column, 1, 62
Column width, 10, 62
Combined graphs, 48
Computer systems, 6
Contents, 9, 24, 62
Cursor, 6, 62

Database, 53, 63
Decimal values, 9
Default values, 63
Directory, 13, 63
Disk, 13, 63
Displayed values, 9, 10, 24, 63

Editing spreadsheets, 9, 63

Filehandling, 8, 13, 63
Fonts, 10, 63
Footer, 27–28, 63
Format, 7, 32, 63
Formula, 7, 8, 63
Freezing information, 50
Functions, 8, 12, 25, 51–52, 63

Global instructions, 64
Graphs, 43–48, 64
Grid lines, 1, 26–27, 64

Header, 27–28, 64
Hidden cells, 50, 64
Histograms, 44, 64

Integer values, 9, 64

Labels, 10, 64
Line graphs, 44, 64
Locked cells, 25, 64
Look-up tables, 51

Macros, 64
Menu, 49, 64

Numbers, 7, 9

Operators, 7, 8

Page break, 64
Pictograms, 48
Pie chart, 44–45, 64
Printing, 11, 12, 26–27
Protected cells, 25, 64

Range, 11, 12, 49, 64
Relative cell references, 23, 64
Replicate, 10, 23–24, 64
Row, 1, 64
Row numbers, 1–2

Scatter diagram, 45–46
Scrolling, 4
Sorting, 25
Spreadsheet, 1, 64
   comparisons, 4
   design, 29–30
   packages, 4
   uses, 3
Stacked bar chart, 46
Status line, 64
Stored values, 64

Template, 64
Text, 7, 9
Title, 64

Value, 64

What if?, 12
Wordprocessing, 53
Worksheet (*see* Spreadsheet)